D0558063

# Cotton Patch Rebel

and dialed "0." The operator gave him the number for Koinonia in Americus. Millard was soon speaking with our friend Al Henry who told him that they were forty miles away and we absolutely *must* come visit. It was good to reconnect with Al and Carol. They insisted on us joining them for lunch in the community dining hall. One of the reasons being "because you *must* meet Clarence Jordan."

We were already seated when Clarence came into the community building. Dressed in blue jeans and work boots, his appearance was rather ordinary except for an "up to something" glint in his eyes. Al had saved him a seat right next to us. Well, to say we were captivated by his stories and spiritual insights would be a grand understatement.

After the meal, Millard and I stepped outside. I recall him saying, "Linda, I think we need to find out if they have a place where we can stay. We need to spend more time here to find out more about Koinonia and have a chance to talk more with Clarence." We had never met a man with such deep understanding of what it means to be a Christian. I quickly agreed. There just happened to be a small house less than one hundred feet from where we ate lunch. Our friends seemed thrilled to have us stay longer. Besides, they needed four more hands to help pack and ship pecans.

What we had planned to be a brief visit turned into a month of rich spiritual renewal and enlightenment. A fairly ordinary day turned into the most *extraordinary* day that changed our lives forever.

There was no doubt about it. God had led us to Koinonia and Clarence Jordan. And it was perfect timing because only a few weeks earlier Millard and I had made a

# Foreword

BEGINNING WITH THAT MONUMENTAL time during December of 1965, Millard and I have been sharing Clarence Jordan and Koinonia through books, speeches, letters, media, and any other way possible. Every time, vivid memories would inspire us all over again. That's why I was so pleased when Ann Trousdale asked me to read her book and write the foreword. The following thoughts and experiences I share with you are dear to my heart and reflect some of the ways God's Kingdom has come to this Earth through Clarence Jordan.

When Millard and I awakened on that sunny winter day in Georgia in 1965, the plan was to drive to our home in Montgomery, Alabama. We had been on a two-week vacation in Florida with our two small children.

While eating breakfast in Albany, Millard remembered friends who had moved to a Christian community and he thought perhaps they could be nearby. He spotted a pay phone on the wall of the café, dropped in a dime

# Contents

*"Now faith is the turning of dreams into deeds;*
*it is betting your life on the unseen realities."*

HEBREWS 11:1
(COTTON PATCH VERSION)

*To Sue Graves Stubbs, who always believed in me*
*and*
*To Mariah Neal and James Patterson, because of whom racism*
*could not take root in my soul*
*A.T.*


*To the Koinonia Farm community for allowing me the space,*
*time, resources, and support to participate in this project*
*T. N.*

COTTON PATCH REBEL
The Story of Clarence Jordan

Copyright © 2015 Ann M. Trousdale. All rights reserved. Except for brief
quotations in critical publications or reviews, no part of this book may
be reproduced in any manner without prior written permission from the
publisher. Write: Permissions, Wipf and Stock Publishers, 199 W. 8th Ave.,
Suite 3, Eugene, OR 97401.

Resource Publications
An Imprint of Wipf and Stock Publishers
199 W. 8th Ave., Suite 3
Eugene, OR 97401

www.wipfandstock.com

ISBN 13: 978-1-4982-2015-6

Manufactured in the U.S.A.

# Cotton Patch Rebel

The Story of Clarence Jordan

## Ann M. Trousdale

*Illustrated by Tracy Newton*
*Foreword by Linda Fuller*

RESOURCE *Publications* · Eugene, Oregon

monumental decision to give away our wealth to the poor and begin searching for what God wanted us to do with our lives. We had been terribly mistaken to think that an extremely materialistic lifestyle would bring us abundant happiness. As it was, our six-year marriage nearly ended in disaster. So this was a soul-searching time, a time to begin rebuilding our relationship with each other, with our children and with our Maker. Our friends and most of our family members thought we had lost our minds to give up what we had worked so hard to achieve! But Clarence affirmed our decision, "You cannot serve God and mammon [money]."

Over time, I had heard or read most of the stories Ann Trousdale relates in her book. However, the chronological flow gave more meaning and understanding to the making of "the man." Her book confirms once again that at every stage of Clarence's life, he broke the mold, a man ahead of his time.

Clarence's keenly observant and bright mind was bent on making a difference in God's order of things. A witty storyteller, he could literally keep an audience of two or two thousand captivated for hours. He was quick to give the perfect "Jesus-like" answer even in difficult or threatening situations. His humor could have you rolling one minute and gasping for breath the next.

Clarence especially enjoyed telling Bible stories to children. I remember when he would tell about Moses leading the children of Israel out of Egypt. It seemed like thunder literally rolled out of his mouth when he exclaimed, "LET MY PEOPLE GO!"

We were always amused when Clarence would use some simple illustration to explain something complicated. For example, he would tell us that God is always broadcasting and that we need to extend our "spiritual antenna" so that we can hear and know what God's will is for us beyond our own. "God is broadcasting and relies on us to listen and do his work. Find out what God has going on and sign up!"

Clarence explained that the thrust of the Bible is from Heaven to Earth, and not vice-versa. The word "believe" meant "to live by." "Repentance" does not mean to feel sorry for getting caught doing something wrong. It means to change . . . change like how a caterpillar goes through a complete and total change in order to become a butterfly. He surmised that this is what we must do if we want to become God's people. Change our ways, our style of life, our values as well as our way of thinking. We must be transformed into a new creature in Christ. "No longer be a 'caterpillar.' Be God's 'butterfly.'" Our heads would be swimming at the end of the day!

Clarence wasn't shy about discussing controversial topics. He had a lot to say about peace and expressing love to fellow human beings, even those who may want to cause harm. One day a man confronted Clarence, yelling, "You people are cowards and shirking your patriotic duties because you won't fight." Clarence responded, "Hey, wait a minute fellow, there must be some misunderstanding. We here at Koinonia are *big* fighters!" The fellow was speechless. Clarence continued. "We are big fighters but *we* choose the weapons." Clarence explained that when a person or a country does something to harm us like pointing a gun, a tank, or a bomb at us, we can choose the weapon we fight with. We can "fight" with love and non-violence. The bad thing about returning evil for evil is that it usually only escalates a battle, producing more casualties. This is not an exact quote but he would say something like, "We can only break the cycle of violence by fighting evil with acts of love. We here at Koinonia believe this way because Jesus teaches us this way in the Bible."

Day in and day out we saw Clarence living the life of a disciple and inspiring thousands of others to do likewise. Like Jesus, Clarence Jordan affected people powerfully. One couldn't be around him and not be affected one way or another. Many people, just as Millard and I, considered Clarence Jordan a prophet, but he was every bit human, too. If he needed a haircut and didn't have time to see a barber, I would usually be the one to trim his hair . . . and his bushy eyebrows. He didn't really care what kind of job I did, he just asked me "to lower his ears."

Clarence was a very gentle man yet always dogged in his faith to Christ. He wouldn't compromise or with-draw, even when a difficult situation confronted him. He believed the essence of Christianity was incarnation; a spoken word without it being acted upon was absolutely meaningless. He was not only a servant in word, but also a servant in deed. Nobody could keep Clarence from carry-ing in people's bags at Koinonia. If a guest came, he would outrun everybody to help unload their belongings and take them to their room.

Millard and I had the privilege of working with Clarence his last year on this earth. Only a few weeks before Clarence died, Phil Gailey, a writer for the *Atlanta*

*Constitution,* was down to interview him about his new book. Millard was with them sitting in the kitchen reminiscing over the things that had happened at Koinonia. Toward the end of the conversation, Phil looked at Clarence and said, "Dr. Jordan, when you get up to Heaven and you are walking down the pearly streets and the Lord comes along and meets you and stops you and says, 'Clarence, old buddy. It's good to see you up here. I wonder if you could tell me in the next five minutes what you did down on Earth. You know, how did things go?' What would you tell the Lord?" Clarence looked at him and without hesitation said, "Why I'd tell the Lord to come back when he had more time."

Linda C. Fuller

Co-Founder of Habitat for Humanity International and<br>The Fuller Center for Housing

# Prologue

CLARENCE JORDAN DIDN'T SET out to be anybody special. He didn't set out to be the kind of person people would write books about, or plays about, or television documentaries about. He didn't set out to lay the foundations for a project to build houses for poor people that would extend around the world. He didn't set out to get people riled up and angry at him. He started out as a simple small-town boy, born the middle child in a large family in Talbotton, Georgia, in 1912.

It was just that he always saw things differently.

# 1

# The One in the Middle

CLARENCE SAT ON THE back step, his chin in the palm of his hand. The day was bright and hot. Flies buzzed around his ears. He absent-mindedly swatted at them, but he didn't pay them any attention. He was deep in thought.

Suddenly the screen door slammed behind him. Bare feet pelted down the wooden step and took off across the back yard. Clarence looked up. It was Frank and Buddie, headed to the Hog Hotel. Clarence jumped up, grabbed his cap and raced after his brothers down the road and out of town. The boys had built a tree house in the tallest hickory tree they could find, on a hilltop overlooking the river. It was seventy-five feet up and it was a long climb to get there, but once you made it, you could see for miles—the farms across the river and when you turned around, the rooftops of the town of Talbotton: the houses, the schools, the stores, their father's bank. It had taken them the whole summer to build the tree house, hauling the lumber up piece by piece from their uncle's lumberyard.

Once they got the stepboards nailed into place, they began taking larger pieces up the tree to make a platform. When there was a big enough platform to stand on, they rigged up a rope pulley to bring larger pieces of timber up. It was the grandest tree house anybody had ever seen. They even put railings up around it so they could sit and lean back and survey the countryside.

Clarence was just starting up the tree after Frank and Buddie when out of the corner of his eye he saw little George at the edge of the clearing. George was looking up at the tree house, his eyes wide, his mouth open in astonishment. It was the first time George had tagged along with them that far away from home. George was just five, too small to climb the tree on his own. Only one thing to do. Clarence called George over and stooped down in front of him. "Climb on," he said. George flung himself onto Clarence's back and wrapped his arms around his brother's neck. "Hang on tight," Clarence said, and started up the tree. George's arms gripped tighter and tighter the higher they went, and Clarence was almost out of breath when they made it to the platform and George slid off his back.

Frank and Buddie were sprawled out, their backs against the railing. George edged over next to Frank. He sat back looking out at the countryside, a wide smile breaking across his face. Clarence sat down next to Buddie. It felt a little bit cooler up here. A slight breeze drifted through, setting the leaves to dancing. Around them on the floor were scattered tin cans, a slingshot, pieces of rope, scraps of board, an old snake skin, a bird's nest–all the things their mother would never allow to clutter their rooms. She wasn't running a hog hotel, she said. So they made their own.

"Reckon I'll string telephone wire up here next," said Frank. "I figured out how we can do it." Frank was already twelve, and Buddie was ten. There wasn't anything Frank and Buddie couldn't do once they set their minds to it, it seemed to Clarence. Stick-to-it-iveness just seemed to run in the family.

Clarence's father had started both the bank and the general store in Talbotton; the buildings were connected. When the boys saw their father step out of the bank, lock the door and lock the door of the general store, they knew it was time to head home for supper.

When the meal was over and the family dispersed, Clarence went back out to sit on the back step, his "thinking place." It was that time of evening when night begins to take over from day. The crickets had commenced their loud chorus, but Clarence hardly noticed. His mind went back to what he had been trying to figure out earlier in the afternoon. There was something that wasn't right. Again that day he had seen little black kids rummaging through white people's garbage bins, pulling out a piece of rotten fruit, a crust of bread, a chicken bone to gnaw. They were hungry. And they were dirty. Their clothes were ragged. The words of the song he learned in his Baptist Sunday school came to him:

> Jesus loves the little children,
> All the little children of the world.
> Red and yellow, black and white,
> They are precious in his sight.
> Jesus loves the little children of the world.

If Jesus loved these children, why were they so hungry and dirty? Did God have favorite children? That's not what the song said. Clarence couldn't figure it out.

It was in the fall of that year, the year Clarence turned eight, that he came down with scarlet fever. It started off like a bad cold or a maybe a case of the flu, but when his mother saw his bright red tongue and the red spots on his chest, she called the doctor. Scarlet fever was a dangerous, contagious disease. The medicines to treat scarlet fever hadn't been developed in those days; people had died from it. Mr. Jordan and the other children moved out of the house to stay with relatives.

Mrs. Jordan brought a nurse from the nearby city of Macon to help her take care of Clarence. They took turns sitting by his bedside, Mrs. Jordan telling Clarence stories about her growing up years in Talbotton, and moving 'way out in Oregon for a while as a child. Clarence lay still and listened to her stories, but he grew worse and worse. One day they thought he was dying and his mother broke down and began to cry. That was when Clarence found out that his mother had lost three newborn babies, two before Frank was born and one between Buddie and Clarence. The thought of losing Clarence was too much for her to bear. Eventually the fever broke, and Clarence began to get better. But the bond that formed between Clarence and his mother was never to be broken. He became her favorite, and all the children knew it. But they didn't begrudge it, as Frank was later to say. They weren't jealous. That was just the way it was.

That was also the beginning of Clarence's "loner" ways. Clarence was the middle child–behind Frank and Cornelia and Buddie and older than George and Bob and John. During his long recovery, Clarence found that he liked spending time alone, reading or just thinking. He taught himself how to play the piano and the trumpet and how to use a typewriter, not by the hunt-and-peck method but using all ten fingers. It was a skill that would come in handy when he grew to be a man. And he listened. He listened to what his father said, to what Cornelia said, to what his brothers said. As he began to feel stronger, if he didn't agree with them, he told them why. It didn't matter which one he argued with, up the line or down the line–somehow he always seemed to come up with a different view, and he would argue his point into the ground. He wouldn't let it go. They took to calling him Grump. Clarence didn't mind. He made a joke of it. Sometimes he signed his school papers "Grump Jordan."

Nobody in town had to be told how to pronounce "Jordan"—*Jerd'n*—Talbotton was full of Jordans. The cousins would come over and they'd go plundering fruit trees or pecan trees, or playing kick-the-can. People used to complain that the town was just over-run with Jordans.

Talbotton was a small town located in western Georgia. Clarence's family was better off financially than many of their neighbors. The Jordan children were among the few children in town who had shoes to wear to school, and their mother insisted that they wear them. So they started off to school, properly shod, and then along the way they stopped, hid the shoes under a bush, and went to school bare-footed like the other kids. They didn't want to show off, and, besides, it just felt better to have your feet free, to wiggle your toes if you felt like it. On the way home from school they stopped, dusted off their feet, and put their shoes back on. Mrs. Jordan thought it was remarkable that they outgrew their shoes before the shoes were hardly worn at all.

Clarence's father owned one of the first cars in Talbotton. On Sunday afternoons he would take the family for a drive. As the family grew, the car became more and more crowded. Once a visitor in town commented to a neighbor how nice that Mr. Jordan was, taking all the neighborhood children for a ride. The neighbor laughed, "Those aren't neighborhood children–they're all his children!" Later Clarence joked that the car was so crowded that the older boys had to get out and run alongside it. People almost believed him.

One day in 1927, the year Clarence turned fifteen, the Jordans' house burned to the ground. The family got out safely, but they had to stay with relatives until a new house, a large two-story brick house, could be built across the street. Mr. and Mrs. Jordan planned five bedrooms, one bedroom for them, one bedroom for Cornelia and three bedrooms for the six boys, two to a room. But none of the boys wanted to share a room with Clarence. He was the kindest and most tender-hearted of the children, and he could be a lot of fun, but he argued so much. Nobody wanted to listen to Clarence argue all night. So when the house was completed, there were five bedrooms all right, one for Mr. and Mrs. Jordan, one for Cornelia, one for Frank and Buddie, a big bedroom for George and Bob and John, and a small one for Clarence. Which suited him just fine. There was always something going on with such a big family, but Clarence liked to be alone too. It gave him time to think. Some of the things he thought about other folks didn't seem to pay much attention to.

## 2

# Just a Little Bit Different

THE COUNTY JAIL WAS only a hundred yards from the Jordans' back door. On many evenings chain gangs, in their black-and-white striped prison uniforms, would be camped out on the jailhouse yard. During the day they had worked along the roadways clearing brush, shuffling along, their ankles shackled together by short heavy chains to keep them from running away. The warden, mounted on a horse, a rifle in the crook of his arm, kept watch over them. In the evening they would be brought to the jail to spend the night.

From the time he was a young boy, Clarence had been interested in these rough, rowdy men, and he would often walk over to visit with them. He made friends with the jail cook, who would give him a piece of cornbread and fatback, and he'd sit and talk to the convicts. Most of them were black, and he got to know several of them by name. He found out that a lot of them were in prison because they had stolen something from white people–a ham or a chicken to feed their families. They'd gotten caught, and they couldn't afford to pay a lawyer to take their case, so they were thrown in prison for years.

More and more Clarence realized just how differently white people and black people lived. They went to separate schools and churches and lived in separate neighborhoods. Some of the streets in the black neighborhood weren't paved, and when it rained they would be muddy and when it was dry they would be dusty. Most of the houses were just shanty houses, drafty and unpainted. Black people weren't allowed to eat in white people's restaurants or use the same bathrooms white people used in public places. There were even separate water fountains for black and white people. Most of the black people Clarence knew worked for white people, as maids or cooks or yard men. When they came to work, they came to the back door, not the front door.

One evening it all came to a head for Clarence. The family was gathered in the living room after supper, the older children doing their homework, Mr. Jordan reading the newspaper and Mrs. Jordan tending to baby John, when there came a knock at the front door. Mr. Jordan opened it, and there stood a black man delivering clothes from the dry cleaner's. Mr. Jordan chastised the man for coming to the front door, and instructed him to go to the back door. Clarence felt his face turn hot with embarrassment. When the man had gone, Clarence laid into his father. Why couldn't a black man come to the front door? Why did his father have to humiliate the man? Wasn't he just doing his job? Mr. Jordan rolled his eyes and looked at the other children. Grump was at it again–always arguing. Always seeing things differently. He let Clarence finish his argument. "Son, you ought to be a lawyer," he said, "you like to argue so much," and went back to his paper.

Like most white Southerners in the early twentieth century, the Jordan family did not challenge the system of racial separation—segregation, it was called. They were kind and generous to the black people who worked for them. Flora Belle, their housekeeper, had worked for the family since before Frank was born and was to stay with them for fifty-six years. Such loyalty must mean that she was content with her life, they reasoned. The fact that white people stood so much to gain from maintaining an unfair social system was not acknowledged or discussed. But even as a young boy, Clarence, with his in-born ability to see a different side of an issue, recognized the unfairness of it. The resolve to do something about it grew as he grew to adulthood; the question was which path he would take to try to make things better.

Once Clarence finished high school, the family assumed he would go to college and then to law school. He'd make a good lawyer. He was always able to see a point that nobody else saw, and was able to argue the point to what seemed to him its logical conclusion. And Clarence did consider becoming a lawyer. But those Sunday afternoon drives had introduced him to the condition of the share-cropper families who lived on the farmlands outside Talbotton. There were many share-croppers who were white, but most of them were black. They worked hard, but somehow they weren't able to make the land produce enough to share the crops they raised with the landowner and still have enough left over for themselves. They seemed caught in a never-ending cycle of hard work and hunger, hunger and hard work. Maybe better farming methods could help them produce better crops and have a better life, Clarence thought. Then they wouldn't have to steal to feed their families. That was the idea that prompted him to major in agriculture at the University of Georgia in Athens after he graduated from high school in 1929.

His father was disappointed. "If you want to be a farmer," he said, "why go to school? I'll buy you a mule and you can start right now." But Clarence wanted to be a scientific farmer, to bring the best agricultural practices back home so he could improve the lot of poor farmers. Although he had hoped Clarence would study law, Mr. Jordan supported Clarence through his four years in agricultural school. But his education wasn't to end there.

3

# A Calling

ATHENS, GEORGIA, WAS LIKE nothing Clarence had ever seen. The town had been built in the rolling hills of central Georgia. The Oconee River ran right alongside the town, and in the residential section little brooks and creeks bubbled through gardens of beautiful houses, homes of planters and bankers and university professors. And downtown there wasn't just one general store and one bank, like the ones the Jordans had in Talbotton. There were three banks, and lots of stores: drugstores, hardware stores, a "department store" where shoes and clothing and jewelry were sold, a bookstore, and even a public library. On the main street downtown stood the arched front gate of the University, opening onto an enormous park-like lawn, called the "quad." Three sides of the quad were lined with handsome two-story brick buildings. One building was the administrative building where all the business of the university was taken care of; others were classroom buildings or dormitories where students lived.

After Clarence got settled into his dormitory room, he went to the administrative building to register for classes. Long lines of students stood at tables, waiting to sign up for the classes they wanted to take. There were classes in every possible subject, from English and foreign languages and journalism to chemistry and physics, to business to forestry and agriculture. Clarence headed first for the College of Agricultural and Environmental Sciences.

Going away to college brought Clarence out of his loner ways. He was on his own for the first time, not just "the one in the middle." His new friends saw him for himself, not as one of the "Jordan boys." At seventeen, he was ready to see how well he could fly by himself.

Everywhere Clarence looked there was something new and interesting to do. There was a debate team, where students practiced arguing different sides of a question. He was good at arguing, so he joined the debate team. There was the literary society, where you read and discussed good books and learned how to write well. He wanted to do that, so he joined the literary society. There was the drama club that put on plays. He hadn't done much drama back home in Talbotton, but he thought he'd enjoy that, so he joined the drama club. Then there was the band. He was sure they could use another trumpet player. He joined the band. Clarence had been brought up going to church and studying the Bible, so he joined the Baptist Student Union and the Young Men's Christian Association. He saw that most of the parties at the university were held at special clubs called fraternities. He joined one of those. Clarence hadn't had much opportunity to dance with girls in Talbotton, but he seemed to be a natural at it. He soon earned a reputation with the girls as a good dancer; all the girls wanted to dance with Clarence Jordan.

And there was more. In those days every male student at the University of Georgia was required to join the Reserve Officers Training Corps (ROTC) their first two years. The idea was that even though the country was not at war, there needed to be young men "on reserve," trained to go to war if war should break out. So all the male students received basic training for two years. They learned the history of the military all the way back to Greek and Roman times. They learned all about military courtesy— how to salute, whom to salute, when to salute, and how to say "sir" to superior officers. They learned how to march in parades and ceremonies. They learned how to shoot a rifle and how to read military maps. They learned basic first aid so they could help a fellow soldier if he got wounded. They learned about military tactics—how to move troops, plan attacks, and defend themselves during a war. Boys could stop at the end of two years or they could volunteer for two more years. If they stuck with it for all four years, at graduation they would be commissioned an officer. Signing on for these two extra years also meant that if the country went to war they would be obligated to report for active duty.

Clarence was offered the choice of joining the infantry (to fight on foot) or the cavalry (to fight on horseback). Clarence signed on for the cavalry. A soldier mounted on a fine horse, armed with a sword and a pistol—that was the dream of many Southern boys. In those days people still fought on horseback; tanks and armored trucks were still in the early stages of development. They would replace horses in the next World War, but when Clarence was in college, the idea of being a soldier on horseback was about as exciting a prospect as a boy could imagine. At the end of his first two years, Clarence liked the idea so much he signed up for the second two years, and when he came home that summer he proudly showed his family the boots and spurs that were part of his cavalry uniform.

During his college years, Clarence began to put on some height. His father was a man of rather short stature, and by the time Clarence finished high school he was just a little taller than his daddy. But every year when Clarence came home from college for summer vacation, he had grown another couple of inches. He finally grew to be six feet, two inches in height, which is not unusual today but was considered very tall back then.

Clarence's college years were full and happy ones. With all of his extra-curricular activities, it's a wonder his grades didn't suffer, but he studied hard and made good grades—good enough for him to be invited to join the Agricultural Honor Society, a club for the top students in agriculture. And it soon became clear that Clarence was a natural leader. At the beginning of his senior year, he was elected editor of the student agricultural newspaper and state-wide president of the Baptist Student Union. But in the middle of his senior year, Clarence found himself questioning his old desire to teach poor people how to farm better. Having a comfortable life was good, he thought, but somehow that didn't seem to be enough. There was more to life than food and clothing. He saw people who had plenty of food and plenty of clothes, who were still not satisfied. There was something missing in their lives. What was it? One day, when he was reading his Bible, the words jumped out at him: "Man does not live by bread alone but by every word that comes from the mouth of God." That was it. People need more than just plenty to eat, they need a spiritual dimension in their lives, a way of living in relationship with God. After almost four years of college study, Clarence realized that he didn't want to do what he had set out to learn how to do. But the old stick-to-it-iveness kicked in and he went ahead and finished the degree in agriculture anyway.

The summer after graduation, Clarence attended a six-week ROTC camp in northern Georgia for more training to be an officer in the cavalry. He took his Bible with him, and began to memorize portions of Scripture. In these days, there are many translations of the Bible available to read, but in Clarence's day the only one that was commonly used was the King James Version. It was written in 1611, and used the old-fashioned language of that time. One day Clarence memorized a passage from the fifth chapter of Matthew's Gospel, when Jesus said:

> Ye have heard that it hath been said: An eye for an eye and a tooth for a tooth. But I say unto you, that ye resist not evil: but whosoever shall smite thee on thy right cheek, turn to him the other also . . . Ye have heard that it hath been said, Thou shalt love thy neighbor, and hate thine enemy: But I say unto you, Love your enemies, bless them that curse you, do good to them that hate you, and pray for them which despitefully use you, and persecute you: That ye may be the children of your

Father which is in heaven: for he maketh his sun
to rise on the evil and on the good, and sendeth
rain on the just and on the unjust.

The language might have been old-fashioned, but
Clarence understood what Jesus was saying. The very
day he memorized this passage from Scripture, it happened that a part of the ROTC training was to take place
in a wooded area where cardboard and straw dummies
had been set up to represent enemy soldiers. Years later,
Clarence described what happened: "We were supposed
to gallop through the woods with our pistols and sabers.
We were to shoot our pistols at the cardboard dummies
and stick the straw dummies with our sabers. Every time
I would shoot at one of those cardboard dummies, that
verse, 'But I say unto you, love your enemies . . .' would
flash through my mind. I tried to swap places in my mind,
where I would be the dummy and he would be the one on
the horse. At that moment I saw the conflict between the
mind of Jesus and the mind of the commanding officer. It
was crystal clear that this Jesus was going one way and I
another. Yet I called myself his follower."

When Clarence broke into the open, he got off his
horse, walked up to the commanding officer, and with-
drew from the cavalry. The officer suggested that Clarence
might want to be a chaplain instead, a preacher to soldiers
who were fighting. But Clarence said that that would be
worse than ever. He couldn't encourage other people to do
what he wouldn't do himself.

So here was Clarence, at twenty-one years of age,
choosing not to do the two things he had spent four years

in college learning how to do. What direction could he find for his life? He went to North Carolina on a church retreat, and there he heard what seemed to him the voice of God saying, "My child, I want you to preach for me." Those words were to change Clarence's life forever.

*4*

# A Shared Dream

IF GOD WAS CALLING him to be a preacher, Clarence knew he would have to go to seminary to be trained to be a preacher. His grades were good enough for him to be admitted to Southern Baptist Seminary in Louisville, Kentucky, one of the best Baptist seminaries in the country. People who are going to be preachers need to know the Bible inside and out, and that meant three years of studying the Bible in a very focused way. Clarence took courses in the Old Testament, which is the Jewish portion of the Bible, and the New Testament, which records the words and actions of Jesus and tells about the early church. Then there were courses on particular sections of the Bible, like the Torah, the first five books of the Bible; or the four Gospels, the first four books of the Christian Testament. Then there were courses that focused on just one book of the Bible, like Genesis or the Gospel According to St. John.

Seminary students were also required to take courses in Hebrew, the original language of the Jewish portion of the Bible, and in Greek, the original language of the

Christian Testament. The letters of both Hebrew and Greek are different from the letters of the English alphabet. So to learn Hebrew or Greek, a person first had to learn a whole new alphabet, and once they had learned the alphabet, they had to learn new vocabulary and the grammar of each language–how to form the past and future tenses of verbs, the plurals and possessives of nouns, all of that. Greek is read from left to right, the way we read English, but Hebrew is read from right to left. Reading backwards takes some getting used to! Then there was no punctuation in the original biblical languages and so you had to figure out where sentences stopped and started from what would look like just a stream of words. It took a long time to learn Hebrew and Greek, but Clarence stuck with it, and the more he studied Greek the more excited he became about getting beyond other people's translations, to be able to read stories about Jesus and Jesus' sayings for himself as they had first been written. As he said, "I wanted to root myself firmly in the teachings of Jesus, in the Greek New Testament, to get it fresh from the stream."

The more Clarence read the New Testament in the original Greek, the more clearly he saw how much Jesus himself was concerned about poor people. He was always making friends with people who were the outcasts of society and even sat down to have meals with them. This shocked the religious leaders of Jesus' day. Jesus touched people who were considered untouchable or unclean and cured their diseases. He spoke to these people in a way that gave them hope, that let them see how much God cared for them. These teachings of Jesus were just like Clarence's own deepest feelings, the way he had felt since he was a little boy, about the equality of all people in God's sight.

Clarence's father had been able to pay Clarence's way through the University of Georgia, but with all the other children to educate he wasn't able to pay for Clarence's seminary expenses. So Clarence looked for work. He soon became a popular "supply preacher," going on Sundays to poor churches that couldn't afford to pay for a preacher full-time. He also preached in hospitals and orphanages. He saw that it wasn't just in the country that people were ragged and dirty and hungry; poor people lived in the city too.

On his many trips to the seminary library, Clarence began to notice a tall, blond blue-eyed girl who worked at the circulation desk. Her name was Florence Kroeger. Clarence saw that there was something special about Florence. As another student put it, Florence "always carried her head just a little higher and had just a little more substance than other girls." Clarence began to find excuses to go to the library just so he could see Florence.

Finally he got up the nerve to ask her out on a date. They found they had a lot in common. Besides having strong opinions of her own about helping poor people and equality between black people and white people, Florence had a spirit of adventure–qualities Clarence admired, and qualities that were to come in handy in the years ahead. They fell in love and married the summer Clarence graduated from seminary.

Clarence wanted to learn everything he could about Jesus from the original Greek, so he and Florence decided to stay on at Southern Baptist Seminary for Clarence to get a PhD—the highest degree you can get–in New Testament Greek. Clarence now took two part-time jobs, one as pastor of a small church in a nearby town, and the other teaching at a seminary that trained African-American preachers. In the last year of his PhD studies, the Jordans had their first child, Eleanor. Clarence wanted to spend as much time as he could with Florence and the new baby, and he gave up his job at the church, but then he was asked to be director of a Baptist mission center in an inner-city neighborhood in Louisville where mostly poor black people lived. He and Florence felt that he couldn't pass up such an opportunity. He took the job, and it turned out that he learned a lot of things that he would use later in his life's work.

One thing he realized was that living in a city wasn't any solution to poverty. Many of the poor people Clarence worked with in these slums, as they were called, had come to the city to flee the poverty of share-cropping in the South. But the city hadn't offered them a better life, maybe even a worse one. The slums were dirty and squalid–no open fields to look at or for children to play in–and for many people there were no jobs to be found in the city either.

Clarence wanted to make the Baptist mission center a place where the neighborhood people could not only get help but also a place where they would like to come and spend time so they could get to know each other. The people who ran the missions were well-off white people. Clarence didn't think white people who lived in other parts of town could really know what people in the poor neighborhoods needed, so he asked black people from the neighborhood to join the white people on the committees that ran the mission. He showed films and brought in visiting preachers and choirs to give concerts. He did such a good job running the mission center that when he received his PhD in 1939, he was asked to stay on as the full-time director of missions. He and Florence decided that he would take the job, and they stayed on another year.

Now Clarence could really get to work on the mission center. He had seen that the children in the neighborhood didn't have any clean places to play, and some of them didn't have any toys. So he developed a playroom in the mission center and a toy library, where children could borrow toys to play with at home. He started clubs for the older boys and girls and a club for mothers so they could get out of the house and have some fellowship. He set up a food pantry where people could come to get food if they ran out of food at home. He started Bible study programs for adults and vacation Bible school and a summer camp for children. Soon the mission center became the center of neighborhood life. People were always there for one reason or another. He organized pot luck suppers where black people and white people sat at the same tables for meals. Today that is common practice, but in those days it was revolutionary, and it brought criticism of Clarence from some of the religious leaders in Louisville. He didn't let it stop him, though.

In his own study of the Bible, Clarence could see that the way Jesus' followers were called to live was different from the way many Christians did live. For one thing, Jesus saw that all people were equal as children of God. As Clarence well knew, most people in the South did not live that way. White people liked to believe that they were better than black people. For another thing, Jesus didn't tell his followers that the best way to live was to make all the money they could and not care about the needs of people who had less money. Jesus called his followers to live simply, to share what they had with others, and to trust that God would take care of their needs. And third, Jesus didn't tell his followers to go to war and kill other people. He taught them to be loving and peaceful and kind, even to people who were not kind to them.

A dream began to grow in Clarence's heart, a dream of forming a community where people lived together in just that way. A community modeled after the first-century church, where all the members gave to the community according to their ability and received from the community according to their need. It would be a place of nonviolence and of racial equality, where people shared meals together and worshiped together and studied the Bible together. Such a place would be a witness to God's love and how God wanted people to live. If there were a community where people really lived like that, surely other people would like what they saw and would want to live that way themselves.

It seemed to him that the city, with its dirty, crowded slums and lack of work would not be the best place to try the kind of community he had in mind. After all, if the people who had moved to the slums could have had better lives on the farms, they wouldn't have had to come to the city in the first place. Maybe the kind of community he wanted to start would be better started on a farm, where everybody could find work of some kind.

About that time he came across an article written in a Baptist newsletter by a man named Martin England. Martin and his wife Mabel had been missionaries in Burma, a small country in Asia now called Myanmar. They had recently been called back to the United States because of wars breaking out over there. In this article Martin had written about a place where a small group of people lived side by side, contributing to the community according to their abilities, trusting the Spirit of God to break down any barriers of race or social class among them and to take care of their needs as they shared all things in common. Clarence was amazed. Here was somebody who thought like he did. Martin had even begun to study agriculture, thinking that such a community might be built on a farm.

In the fall of 1941, Clarence and Martin both attended a meeting of the Fellowship of Reconciliation in Louisville. They began to share their ideas of how people could live together in peace, without violence. The more they talked the more they got excited about finding a way to make their dream come true.

They decided that the best place for their experiment would be in the deep South. That's where they saw the greatest need–and the greatest potential. They were both Southerners themselves—Martin had grown up in South Carolina–and they knew they would run into some resistance in the South, especially to their ideas about racial equality. But they thought that being from the South would be an advantage; they wouldn't be outsiders bringing in something foreign. They would begin quietly, be good neighbors, and gradually win people over by being a witness to God's way for people to live.

The first step would be to find some farmland. Ordinarily if people were setting out to be farmers, they would try to find the best, most fertile land they could find so they could make a lot of money off the land. But that wasn't what the Jordans and Englands were trying to do. They thought of the farm they would buy as a "demonstration plot," a place that would first of all be a witness to the way God wanted people to live. They came up with a few requirements for the land itself: it had to be in the deep South, in an area where the proportion of black people to white people was similar to other parts of the South. There needed to be a large share-cropping population in the area, and the land itself needed to be typical farmland for the South, with soil that had been depleted and eroded by poor management. They didn't want their experiment to succeed because they had started off with good land to begin with: they wanted a typical Southern farm. Clarence couldn't help realizing that this idea fulfilled his old childhood dream of helping poor farmers, but adding "more than bread alone" to share. He could teach people about God while he was teaching them about farming.

# 5

# Breaking Ground

IN THE LATE SUMMER of 1942 the Jordans and the Englands set out in search of a farm to buy. They had driven through miles and miles of countryside in the deep South when Clarence's brother Frank, who still lived in Talbotton, told them about a 400-acre farm for sale located in Sumter County, Georgia, just outside the town of Americus, only sixty miles south of Talbotton. The farm was divided by a two-lane road, as many farms had been divided when new roads were built. There was one old, dilapidated four-room house, an old barn made out of sheet metal, and a sagging tool shed. The land was mostly flat, but back behind the farmhouse there was an area that rose to a gentle hill. A creek, the Muckaloochee, ran through the property. The land was almost treeless, with slightly eroded soil and broken-down fences. It seemed right.

They gave the owner a few dollars to hold the land until they could come up with the down payment, a percentage of the total cost that would give them a start. They would pay the rest of the cost over time. They didn't have enough money for the down payment themselves, but both Clarence and Martin were familiar with the way Baptist churches raised money for special missions. They would make up a brochure to send out to churches and to people they knew describing their project and asking for donations.

During his work with the mission center in Louisville, Clarence had met a businessman named Arthur Steilberg. Arthur immediately took to Clarence. He liked Clarence's sincerity and his enthusiasm. He was interested in Clarence's idea for a community and had told Clarence that he'd give Clarence some money for the project the next time he made a good business deal. Right at that time it happened that Arthur did make a lot of money in his construction business, and when Clarence got back to Louisville, Arthur handed him an envelope. Clarence knew that Arthur was a generous man, and he expected a gift of maybe $400 or $500. When he opened the envelope, he saw with amazement that it was much more than that. Arthur had given him $2300, the exact amount of the down payment. They were on their way.

They named the farm "Koinonia," (pronounced koy-no-*nee*-ah), the Greek word for "community." There was a lot of work to do before any kind of community could be formed there, though: the old house wasn't fit to live in, the other buildings needed to be repaired, and the land needed to be tended. While they were in Louisville making plans for the move, the Jordans' second child, Jim, was born.

They decided that Clarence and Martin would move to the farm in November, camp out in the house, and begin getting it ready for the families to move into. Mabel and the three England children, John, Beverly, and Jeanette, would stay behind in Kentucky, and Florence and Eleanor and baby Jim would go to Talbotton, to stay in the old Jordan family home.

In 1941, the year before they bought the farm, the United States had gone to war with Germany and Japan, in what became known as World War Two. Being at war meant that most of the building materials in the country were devoted to the war effort, and Clarence and Martin had a hard time getting building permits or supplies for the farm. They patched the house up enough for Mabel and the England children to join them in December, but it turned out that the old house would never really be fit for a family to live in. For one thing, the only water in the house came from a pipe that ran from a well in the yard through a hole in the kitchen wall. Besides that, the house was drafty and hard to keep warm in winter. But even worse, it was over-run with fleas. There were no flea sprays in those days, and fleas would bite people right along with dogs and cats, leaving hundreds of little red itchy spots. It was especially bad if the fleas got into the mattresses; they would bite people all night. Mabel learned that farm wives got rid of fleas in their beds by using mothballs, hard round balls made of chemicals that have a strong, pungent odor that fleas don't like. Mabel bought several boxes of mothballs in town, got a hammer, smashed the mothballs and put the mothball flakes under the bottom sheets. That made getting into bed a little crunchy and smelly, but at least they weren't scratching fleas all night. Even so, the house was no place for a new-born baby, and Florence and the two Jordan children stayed in Talbotton through the first winter.

That turned out to be a good thing for another reason. That winter all three England children came down with measles, mumps, and chicken pox, one illness after the other. Mabel stayed up night and day caring for them until she came down with the mumps herself. Then she had to go to bed and Martin took over as nurse and cook. Martin didn't know much about cooking. For supper he would mix together whatever leftovers there were in a big pot and called it "Muckaloochee Special," after the creek that ran through the property. Mabel and the children and Clarence were hungry enough to eat it.

After a miserable winter Clarence was finally able to get a permit to buy supplies to build a utility building, a "shop" as he called it, a big room where all the tools and supplies for the farm could be kept. They added a second story that was to become the home for both families. Finally, in the spring of 1943, Florence and Eleanor and Jim joined Clarence and the Englands at Koinonia Farm. Eleanor and Beverly England were both five years old and they soon became good friends.

The Jordans and Englands believed that they were called to share all things in common as the early church did, so they established a "common purse," into which all the income was put and out of which they would take money to meet each person's needs. In the beginning, the adults divided the labor. Clarence and Martin worked to get the land ready for farming and Florence and Mabel did the cooking and housekeeping and looked after the five children. Clarence and Martin planted lots of trees–pecan, walnut, apple, peach, fig, pear, plum, and persimmon. It would take years for the pecan trees to mature, but the fruit trees would bear more quickly, giving them enough for themselves and some left over to sell. They didn't have the money to buy a mule, so they borrowed one and began to plow up the hard-packed land.

Once the hard ground had been broken up and it was time to lay out the rows to plant the seed, Clarence and Martin would hitch each other up to the plow, one in front of the plow pulling it and the other behind guiding it. That must have caused quite a few double-takes for anyone casually driving by!

Clarence and Martin thought they knew something about farming, and they did. After all, Clarence had gotten a university degree in agriculture and Martin had studied agriculture a little himself. But they found out that "armchair farming" as they called it—just studying about farming—was a far cry from actually managing a 400-acre farm. Now they needed some practical knowledge, like exactly when was the best time to plant which crops in that particular part of Georgia. Clarence would later joke that in their early days he used to climb up on the rooftop every morning to see what the neighbors were doing. "If they were plowing, we plowed," he said. "If they were planting, we planted." Clarence told that story to poke fun at himself, but he and Martin did have to learn the rhythm of the land. Then they would be able to put their scientific knowledge to work.

At the university Clarence had learned not to plant the same crop in the same field year after year. In the South people had planted cotton that way for generations, and the cotton plants had absorbed all the nutrients, leaving the soil depleted. They decided to plant some cotton, but to rotate it with other plants. One of the crops they decided to plant was peanuts. The nuts themselves grew underground, among the roots, and the whole plant had to be pulled up to get to the nuts. The traditional way to harvest peanuts was to dig up the plants and haul the whole plant to a stationary harvester to separate the nuts from the vines. Clarence studied that process, and came up with a labor-saving solution. He figured out a way to put wheels on the harvester and bring it to the plants, thus eliminating wasted time and energy. Clarence put his intelligence and scientific knowledge to use in another way. It was the general practice to just throw away the empty vines after harvesting the nuts; Clarence realized that the vines could be plowed back into the soil, returning nutrients to the land for the next planting. He knew that the depleted soil in other fields needed to have nutrients added as well. A farmer could buy chemical nutrients and fertilizers at feed and seed stores, but the soil needed to be scientifically analyzed to know which nutrients to add. So Clarence devised a chemistry set for testing the soil to know which nutrients he should add.

With all the cotton and peanuts and fruits and vegetables, there were more crops to harvest than Clarence and Martin could take care of themselves. It wasn't hard to find a local black man who needed work, and they hired the man to help them. In those days it was the custom in the South to pay a black person less than a white person. Clarence and Martin thought this was wrong, and they paid the black worker just as much as they would have paid a white worker.

The brochures that Clarence and Martin had sent out asking for financial support continued to bring in donations. In the Koinonia newsletters, Clarence thanked their supporters and let them know how things were going on the farm. Pretty soon he was writing about poultry farming. In his travels around the countryside, Clarence had noticed that there were no chicken farms. He had studied poultry farming at the University of Georgia, and thought that an egg business could be a good source of income. It could also be something he could teach to other farmers in the area. He wrote about his idea in the newsletter.

One day a big truck drove onto the property. It was loaded with crates and crates of baby chicks, their little heads sticking out between the slats of the crates, cheeping away. A farmer in Virginia had sent them 500 baby chicks. Another friend sent fifty more. Pretty soon, Clarence said, it was like Old MacDonald's farm: here a chick, there a chick, everywhere a chick, chick. They were able to get a permit to build a house for the chickens to keep them safe at night from wild animals and to be a place where the hens eventually could lay their eggs in safety. The chicken house was so sturdy and warm and dry that Mabel joked that she begged Martin and Clarence several times to let her live in the new chicken house. "It didn't leak, it was well heated, and it would seat two thousand!"

Right up the road from Koinonia was the Rehoboth Baptist Church. The Jordans and Englands joined the church, and when the members found out that a new Baptist minister had moved nearby they asked him to preach. They found out what a good preacher Clarence was, how he could make the Bible come alive and spice up his sermons with funny stories that illustrated the point he was making. They asked him to preach again and again. Beverly later recalled that she and Eleanor liked to sit in the front row, where they could be away from their families, out of the reach of the grown-ups. One Sunday when Clarence was preaching he worked in a story about the vanity of a police officer with a new pair of shoes. To show his shoes off the officer found a way to give directions using the shoes. To demonstrate Clarence kicked up his foot and kicked over a basket of flowers standing next to the pulpit. Everybody laughed, but Eleanor and Beverly couldn't stop laughing. They clapped their hands over their mouths and tried to stop, but every time they looked at each other they'd set each other off again. They giggled all through the service, and the adults couldn't get to them without making a scene because they were sitting down in the front row.

Pretty soon word about Clarence's preaching spread, and he was asked to speak at big church meetings and at college youth organizations all over the state and even in nearby Florida. He became such a popular speaker that it wasn't long before he would be asked to speak somewhere most week-ends. The income helped pay farm expenses. Clarence could preach on a lot of subjects, but he would often also tell his audiences about the experiment at Koinonia. The older adult audiences didn't seem to warm to the stories about Koinonia, but the college students were interested and they would ask if they could come visit. There wasn't an extra bedroom, and the students had to sleep on a blanket in the hall or on the kitchen floor. Some would stay a few days, some a week or two, and some stayed for the whole summer.

There was no air conditioning back in those days, and the summer days were hot. The children would find cool places to play under the old farm house or in the shady barn. If their parents were too busy, they could usually persuade one of the visiting students to take them down to Muckaloochee Creek for a cool dip, taking the Englands' water spaniel, Inky, with them, making plenty of noise to scare any snakes or other wild creature away from the swimming hole before they got there! Another cooling-off time came on Sunday afternoons when they would all gather on the lawn for cold watermelon.

That fall Beverly and Eleanor began first grade. John was in third grade, and the three of them would go stand by the roadside every morning to wait for the school bus. There were only white children on the bus, no black children. They had their own school.

By fall of the next year, 1944, the war in Burma was dying down. The Baptist Church's mission office contacted Martin and Mabel, asking them to return to the mission field. It was a hard decision. They had put so much work into Koinonia, but they felt that the primary call on their lives was to foreign mission. Clarence and Florence assured them that they would be able to keep the farm going, and in September, two years after Koinonia was begun, Martin and Mabel and the England children tearfully said good-bye.

6

# Branching Out

FOR THE NEXT FEW years the Jordans were the only family living full-time on the farm. But they weren't lonely. They didn't have time to be lonely. There was always plenty of work to be done, and they were also becoming more and more involved at Rehoboth Baptist Church, leading Sunday school classes and Bible studies for both grown-ups and children. When Clarence was in town and wasn't preaching, he often led the singing.

The farm continued to attract the neighbors' interest. For one thing, they weren't used to seeing a farmyard overrun with chickens. Other farmers might keep a few chickens to help feed their own households, but nobody had any more than that. And those 550 baby chicks grew into a large flock of laying hens who soon were producing eggs. The Jordans built a road-side stand where they could sell the eggs and other farm produce. But soon the hens were laying more eggs than the Jordans could possibly sell from the roadside stand; they were laying enough eggs to sell to grocery stores in Americus and most of Sumter County. Soon it seemed that Koinonia eggs were sold everywhere.

The Koinonia hens produced so many eggs that the neighbors started telling tall tales about them. One story that circulated was that Clarence and Martin had build a special kind of nest with a chute under it that rolled the freshly-laid egg right down into a basket, and when the hen stood up to look at her egg she would think she hadn't laid one after all and would lay another one. But that wasn't true—all Clarence and Martin had done was to apply good farming techniques: feeding the hens well and keeping them warm and dry. And the hens kept on producing.

In 1946 the Jordans welcomed a third child, Jan, into the family. And along with the family, the community grew. Beginning in 1948 other people arrived to join Koinonia, not just as visitors passing through, but as full-time members of the community. The first were young people who had heard Clarence speak at their colleges and who liked his ideas about how people should live together. Willie Pugh, who heard Clarence speak at her college in Mississippi, came to join the community. Next was Harry Atkinson, who had visited Koinonia during his college years. Harry had gone away to seminary and gotten married, and he returned to Koinonia with his wife Allene. Howard Johnson, who had also visited Koinonia while he was in college, finished his studies at Auburn University and arrived one day on his Harley-Davidson motorcycle. Clarence liked the Harley and learned how to ride it. He liked it so much he later borrowed it to ride all the way to Texas for a speaking engagement, almost a thousand miles away. The only part of his face that didn't get dusty and sun-burned was the area around his eyes that were protected by the goggles. He later joked that when he arrived in Texas and took off his goggles and looked in the mirror, he looked like he still had goggles on—white ones, against his dusty, sun-burned face. Fortunately, when it came time to give his talk, his face was back to normal.

Con and Ora Browne were the next people to come. Con was in seminary in Chicago when he heard Clarence speak. One of the qualities that drew Con to Clarence had its roots in Clarence's old argumentative nature, his ability to see a different view and to follow it to what he thought was its logical conclusion. He had honed that ability when he was on the debate team at the University of Georgia. As Con later said, "There was a certain quality about him that melted one into admiration. It was his nature to challenge every idea until he had worked it through and accept or reject it, for he dearly loved to argue–part of his debating experience earlier in life."

When Con finished his studies in 1949, he and Ora and their two children moved to Koinonia. Now Eleanor and Jim and Jan had playmates on the farm again. Soon more children were to arrive. Con and Ora had two more, and Harry and Allene had three. Howard got married and he and his wife Marian had two children. Houses were built to accommodate the new families. Now Eleanor, Jim, and Jan had lots of friends.

From the start, Clarence had wanted to pattern Koinonia on the first-century church as it was described in the Bible. One thing the Bible said was that the members of the early church sold what they had and shared all things in common, everyone giving according to their abundance and receiving according to their need. That was the way the Jordans and Englands had operated, and that was the way Clarence thought Koinonia should continue to operate as it grew. And so when people joined the community they either sold what they had and gave it to the poor, or shared it with the community. All of their earnings went into the common purse. That was hard for some people to get used to, not having money of their own to spend as they liked. But Clarence thought it was important that people trust God and the community to take care of their needs.

Clarence's good farming practices began to pay off. There was enough income from the poultry business and from the sale of cotton and peanuts to buy more land, then a small herd of cattle and some pigs. Soon they were able to buy a tractor to plow the fields and put in more crops. They built a larger road-side stand—a real market—on the main highway to sell their abundant farm produce and eggs. They put in a meat refrigerator and began to sell cuts of beef and pork.

Living on a farm meant that everybody had chores to do. First there were the daily chores: preparing the meals and feeding the chickens and livestock. The big kids learned how to help feed the chickens and take table scraps down to the pig troughs for the pigs. It was Eleanor's job to collect the eggs every day. She didn't like this one bit. There was a big rat snake that lived near the chicken yard and while it kept wild animals away from the hens and was harmless to people, Eleanor didn't like the idea of seeing it come slithering around a corner one day. But collecting eggs was her job and she did it. Another chore for the older kids was to help look after the littler ones. There seemed to be an ever-growing number of children on the farm, with a few babies in diapers, a few learning to walk, and a few wanting to tag along behind the older kids.

There was heavier work too for the grown-ups: plowing, planting, chopping weeds and harvesting the crops. Some of the produce they sold fresh in the market, but some they canned so that it would keep for several months after harvest-time. On a lot of farms at that time women did the indoor work, like cooking and cleaning, and the men did the outdoor work, like plowing and harvesting.

But at Koinonia, sometimes the women took turns with the men in driving the trucks and the tractor, and the men pitched in to help with the canning. With the community growing so large, they built two other houses and a big dining room and kitchen where all the community could meet to share meals together.

Soon baby calves were born. Once the baby calves were old enough to eat grass on their own, they were ready to be weaned from their mothers' milk. But even after a calf is weaned, the mother cow keeps on producing milk for six or seven more months. Clarence and the other men continued to milk the cows every morning until the cows ran dry. There was more than enough milk for the Koinonia children. As Clarence drove around the countryside, he noticed that some of the poor sharecropper families didn't have a cow. He knew that that meant that their children didn't have any milk to drink. He thought of the toy library he had started back in Louisville for families who didn't have any toys for their children. Why not start a cow library? Koinonia had enough milk to be able to share their cows. He put the word out that Koinonia would lend cows to families that didn't have a milk cow. They could keep the cow until she went dry and then bring her back and check out another one. Soon it wasn't unusual to see a farmer, black or white, leading a milk cow along the road, either away from Koinonia to their own houses or back to Koinonia, returning the cow for another.

Helping in this way was good, but Clarence wanted to teach other farmers how to farm better on their own too. The first opportunity came through those 550 donated chicks. Clarence hoped that some of the poor farmers in the area would see the possibility of raising chickens for a money-making business themselves. He invited them to stop by to see the chicken house and to learn how they could start their own flocks. Once they got their flocks started, he taught them how to grade and market their eggs. Soon he was holding regular meetings at Koinonia to teach ways of improving farming. He taught about poultry farming, how to rotate crops, how to fertilize the land.

Both black and white farmers came to learn. They didn't seem to have a problem with sitting in the same room to hear a lecture. But when refreshments were served afterwards, either one group or the other would leave. In those days it was the custom for white people not to eat with black people; sharing a meal or even sharing refreshments with black people seemed like an admission that black people were equal to white people, and they didn't want to do that. For their part, black people had learned not even to try to socialize with white people. So if the white people stayed for refreshments the black people would leave, and if it looked like the black people were staying the white people would leave. Clarence noticed this, of course, but he didn't make an issue of it. He and Florence shared the refreshments with whoever stayed.

Friendship and goodwill began to grow between Koinonia and their neighbors. Clarence continued to travel, speaking about Koinonia and "the God Movement," as he called it. More and more people decided they wanted to be a part of the community. By late 1949, there were fourteen adults and twelve children living at Koinonia, and more were on the way. Everything seemed to be going as the Jordans and Englands had hoped; the experiment at Koinonia seemed to be a success. The farm was productive, the community was growing, they were making friends, and Clarence was able to help poor people have better lives. There had been a few bumps in the road, but those first years were happy ones. They didn't know that trouble was soon to come.

## 7

# Trouble Brewing

THE JORDANS AND ENGLANDS had known that some
of their ideas about the way God wanted people to live
wouldn't be popular in Sumter County, especially their
ideas about racial equality and not fighting with your enemy. After all, both Clarence and Martin had grown up
in the South, and they knew Southern ways. They didn't
set out to push their opinions down other people's throats
but hoped that by being good neighbors and practicing
loving-kindness, people would see God's hand in the way
they were living. They wanted Koinonia to be a witness for
the "God Movement."

There had been a couple of disturbing incidents in the
early years, but they seemed to have blown over. The trouble had to do with people's ideas about the relationship between black people and white people. To understand that
relationship in the South, you have to go all the way back
to colonial times, to the early 1700s, when people from
England settled along the Atlantic coast in the American
colonies. In the southern colonies, many of them either

bought large pieces of land or were given large pieces of land by the King of England. The idea was to grow crops to export to England and make a lot of money.

In those days there were also people who would sail large ships to Africa and capture African men, women and children and bring them to the American colonies to be sold as slaves. They were considered the property of the white people who bought them from the slave ships. Slaves didn't have any rights. They were put to work on the plantations, as the big farms were called, and didn't get paid for their work. They lived in rough cabins, often a whole family in one small room. They were given just enough food to keep them going, and had only ragged clothes to wear. They worked from sunup to sundown, and if the white people thought a slave wasn't working hard enough, they would punish him, usually by beating him with a long whip. If slaves tried to escape, the slave holders sent men on horseback after them to bring them back. They would be punished and put to work again. The slaves provided cheap labor for the landowners, and before long the success of the plantations depended on the system of slavery.

In the next century, in the mid-1800s, the American Civil War freed the slaves, and many freed slaves moved to the North. But many stayed on the plantations as share-croppers because farming was the only work they knew how to do. Share-croppers would live on white people's land, work a portion of the land, and give a percentage of the crop they raised to the land-owner. The problem was that they were hardly able to grow enough crops to pay the land-owner and have enough left over to meet their own family's needs. Share-cropping turned out to be not much better than slavery. There were white share-croppers too, white people who were too poor to buy land for themselves, but most of the share-croppers were former slaves.

Most of the white people in the South wanted to keep black people poor and uneducated so that they wouldn't have any choice but to work for them at whatever wage they decided to pay. It wasn't just the plantation owners who thought this way. White people who lived in towns liked to have black people clean their houses and cook for them and take care of their yards. And there were other white people who held the jobs that called for being able to read and write and do arithmetic. They didn't want to have black people competing with them for their jobs or to be able to vote. And because most black people in the South didn't have access to an education, a lot of white people thought they weren't as smart as white people. On almost all levels of white society, white people thought it was to their advantage to keep black people down. They wanted black people to be afraid of what they would do to them if they tried to have a better life.

They formed groups to terrorize black people who wanted to be anything other than servants of white people. The largest of these groups was the Ku Klux Klan, who wore white hooded robes and rode around at night trying to frighten people. They burned crosses in people's yards as a warning. If the people didn't change their ways, the Klan would come back and kidnap the men in the family and take them off and kill them. They killed mostly black people, but they were known to burn crosses in white people's yards and kill white people too, if the white people didn't agree with them. The police didn't do anything about it; if they weren't members of the Klan themselves, they almost surely had a brother or cousin who was. In the South, white people's word was law. Black men learned to hide from the "night riders" and to be very careful in the daytime to make sure they didn't say or do anything that might make white people mad.

White Southerners had many ways of trying to make black people feel inferior. First were the low wages, much lower than they would pay a white person. They would never let a black person come to the front door; black people had to use the back door. They would never sit down to share a meal with black people. They would give black helpers their meals in the kitchen by themselves or out on the back steps. They didn't want black people to be able to vote. And they used language that was disrespectful of black people. They called them "niggers," a term that's not acceptable today. But they used it then if they were ignorant or mean.

That was the social system the Jordans and the Englands moved into in the 1940s. Clarence and Martin didn't want deliberately to offend their white neighbors by going against their customs, but they knew that there were some ways they themselves had to live that they couldn't back down on. One was their belief that God was no respecter of persons, as the scriptures said; that is, God didn't consider some people better than others–and neither would they.

The first incident happened in the very early years, when the Englands were still at Koinonia. It had to do with a black man whom Clarence and Martin had hired to help out on the farm. When lunch-time came, they invited the man to sit down at the table to share the meal just as they would have invited a white man. It wasn't long before word got around Sumter County that the Jordans and the Englands were sitting down for meals with a black man. A group of white people showed up at Koinonia one evening asking for Clarence Jordan. Clarence identified himself, nodding at each one politely. Finally the man who was the spokesperson for the group looked Clarence in the eye, and said, "We understand you been taking your meals with a nigger."

Clarence replied softly, "Well, now, at lunchtime we usually eat with a man we've hired."

The spokesperson jutted out his jaw and said, "We're from the Ku Klux Klan, and we're here to tell you we don't allow the sun to set on anybody who eats with niggers."

Clarence tried to think of a way to respond. He was in a dangerous situation and he knew it. How could he be peaceful and yet not back down on what he thought was right? He glanced at the sun, which was just about to set. All of a sudden he remembered a story from the Bible, when Joshua had made the sun stop in the sky. That was it. Clarence smiled a big smile, and took the man's hand and began to pump it up and down. "I'm a Baptist preacher," he said, "and I just graduated from a Baptist seminary. I read in the Bible that Joshua commanded the sun to stand still in the sky but I never thought I'd meet someone like him in South Georgia! I'm glad to meet you!"

The other man didn't know what to say. He stood there, gawking at Clarence, his hand pumping up and down in the air with Clarence's. Finally all he could think of to say was, "I'm a—I'm a son of a Baptist preacher myself . . ." The other men started talking and laughing, and the anger was broken.

The second incident occurred when Clarence and Martin noticed that school buses came to pick up white children to take them to the white school in town but there were no buses to take black children to the black school. It was a long walk to school in good weather, but in bad weather it was almost impossible. Clarence and Martin thought it was important for the black children to get an education, so when the weather was bad one of them would get in the car and one would get in the truck and drive around to the black people's cabins, pick the children up and take them to school.

The superintendent of schools in Americus was one of the people who didn't want black children to be educated. He wrote a letter to Clarence's father who was very ill at the time, telling Mr. Jordan that Clarence was "endangering his family" through his work at Koinonia, and asking Mr. Jordan to persuade Clarence to move back to Talbotton. One day soon after that, Clarence was passing through Talbotton on his way home from a speaking engagement and stopped for a visit. His father, still very weak, showed Clarence the letter. He was clearly upset by it, worried about Clarence's safety. Clarence was enraged. He drove to Americus, skidded his car to a halt outside the superintendent's office, walked in, grabbed the man by his necktie, picked him up, and told him that if he ever heard about the man's worrying his sick Daddy again he would forget Jesus Christ for fifteen minutes and beat the living daylights out of him. Clarence was later to say that that was one time in his life when he came close to losing his religion. But the superintendent didn't object again, at least not as far as Clarence or his family knew.

Things seemed to calm down for a few years. But then there was Clarence's preaching and teaching. Clarence could preach and teach on many subjects, but his ideas of how he believed God wanted people to live began to creep more and more into his talks. Some of his Southern listeners didn't want to hear about that, and they stopped asking Clarence to come preach. At the same time his reputation was spreading to other parts of the country, and he was asked more and more to speak in the Midwest, or up in the

Northern and Eastern parts of the country, where people did want to hear what Clarence was saying. But finally his own home church, Rehoboth Baptist Church, asked him to stop preaching there.

In August of 1950 an incident occurred at Rehoboth that created a crisis. A young man from India, a country in Asia, came to Koinonia to visit. He was studying agriculture at Florida State University and was interested in the Koinonia experiment. That Sunday he went to church with members of Koinonia. The Baptist Church had a strong interest in foreign missions, and the Koinonia folks thought that the people at Rehoboth would welcome the young man. After all, they supported the Englands in their missionary work in Burma, which was right next to India. But the members of Rehoboth had never been to Burma or to India. They didn't know that people from that part of the world had skin that was darker than their own skin. The church members thought the people from Koinonia had brought one of their black farm hands to church. It was bad enough that the members of Koinonia worked alongside black people and sat down to have meals with them, but they would not be allowed to bring black people to their white church. Not only did the church members not welcome the young man, they refused to speak to him at all.

A couple of days later a car pulled into the Koinonia driveway. Out got a group of men from the church. They asked to see Clarence, and they got right to the point. They told Clarence that the church had decided that Koinonia members were no longer welcome at Rehoboth Baptist Church. Clarence said that he and the others wanted to apologize if they had done anything wrong. The men were all Baptists, who had been brought up to base everything they did on the Bible. Clarence handed one of the men a Bible and asked him to show him where he had gone against God's teaching. The man couldn't think of anything to say, so he handed the Bible to the next man. That man couldn't think of anything to say either and handed the Bible to the man next to him. So it went until the last man was handed the Bible. "Don't give us any of that Bible stuff!" the man shouted and handed the Bible back to Clarence. Clarence suggested that maybe the men should be the ones to leave the church if they didn't care about God's teaching. The men had no answer for that. They turned around, got in their car and left.

Clarence realized that he had won the argument in a sense, but that he needed to find a way to reconcile the issue. A few days later he went to visit three deacons of the church who he thought were friends, but it didn't do any good. The deacons said the church wanted the Koinonia members to leave. That Sunday the church held a special meeting and voted to withdraw membership from Clarence and Florence and the other people at Koinonia. They could no longer go to church at Rehoboth.

# 8

# Fiery Trials

IT WAS HURTFUL TO be turned out of the church, but the
pain was eased somewhat by the small but steady stream
of people from other parts of the country who agreed
with Clarence's teaching and wanted to live out their beliefs at Koinonia. Some were single, some were married,
some brought children. Some came and stayed for a few
months, or for a year or two, but others stayed for years
and years. Con and Ora Browne and their children, who
had arrived in 1949, were to stay for fourteen years. In
1953 Margaret and Will Wittkamper and their three boys,
Billy, Greg, and David, arrived, also to stay for fourteen
years. A fourth boy, Danny, was born a few years later.
Some of the people who came knew a lot about farming,
and others knew just a little, but they were all willing to
work. With so much good help, Clarence was able to buy
more land and increase crop production. The chicken
flock grew to over 4,000 laying hens. They enlarged the
roadside market again.

As Greg Wittkamper later said, Koinonia was a paradise for kids. The open fields and the orchards were good places for camping out. They pretended to be Indians and learned to shoot a bow and arrow. They flew over the rough roads on their bicycles—and learned how to repair the bikes too. There were two horses on the farm, Star, named for the white mark on his forehead, and Danny, who was the gentler of the two. Sometimes the children got to ride double with Clarence on Star or Danny as he

went to check on the crops or the cattle out grazing in the pastures. On summer days the children would load up in the truck and be taken off to Wall's Mill Pond nearby, where there was good swimming and a waterfall to play in. The whole community gathered for meals in the dining hall, good times for visiting and relaxing, with music and singing and dancing after supper. A couple of evenings a week children and parents from nearby farms came for Bible study and refreshments. And Sunday afternoons brought the community members up to Picnic Hill, with everybody singing their way up the hill and back home as the stars came out. On clear nights when the stars were especially bright they'd lie down on the grass, looking up at the stars, as Clarence pointed out the constellations in the heavens above.

For the kids, living at Koinonia was a little like living on an island. You had to leave five days a week to go to school, but once you were back on the island, life was good. Everybody worked together, but they played together too. Their happiness didn't come from any luxuries; there were no fancy toys or clothes. Life was kept as simple as possible. Florence was a good seamstress, and she made many of her family's clothes. She was warm and affectionate with all the children, but she believed in discipline too. Because there were so many flies out in the country, she always kept a fly swatter handy. But flies weren't the only thing she swatted. If a kid misbehaved, or got just a little too rambunctious, Florence would bend over and reach for the fly swatter. Sometimes that was all it took, just bending and reaching, and the kid quickly settled down.

Florence knew how much children like special treats, and especially sweet ones. So she invited the Koinonia children to come to her house one time a day—just one— to get a piece of candy. She seemed to get as much pleasure as they did as their hands hovered over the big bowl until they decided on the piece they wanted.

Since the Koinonia kids couldn't go to Sunday school at Rehoboth Baptist Church, the grown-ups decided to have Sunday school right there on the farm. And even better than at Rehoboth, they could invite black children from neighboring farms to come too. Two black families moved to Koinonia with their children, and now there were eighteen children, black and white, in the community. When summer came Koinonia held Vacation Bible School for black and white children together.

But the more Koinonia flourished, the unhappier the white people in Sumter County became. They didn't want to see Koinonia as a witness to God's Kingdom–they didn't want to see it at all. They liked their segregated way of life. They didn't want to listen to people who said that wasn't the way God intended people to live, that all people were equal in God's sight, that people who had plenty should share with others who didn't have enough. What would happen to their comfortable way of life if black people got the idea they were as good as white people? Who would work their farms and clean their houses and cook their food? They wanted black people to stay in their place.

Then, in 1954 everything changed. The Supreme Court of the United States issued a ruling that rocked the Deep South. The ruling declared that racial segregation in public schools was unconstitutional. That meant that all the "white" public schools had to admit black students. All across the South white people rallied to try to keep black children out of their schools. If black children got an equal education, they would be equally qualified for white people's jobs. They would demand equal pay. The whole Southern way of life would be changed. And right here in Sumter County was a group of people who already lived that way. The local white people decided they had to force the Koinonia leaders to sell the farm and make all the Koinonia people move away from Sumter County.

But how could they do that? They tried three things. The first was to stop the farm from making any money. They would make sure that nobody in Sumter County bought any Koinonia produce. All the white people stopped going to the road-side market to buy food for their families. When the Koinonia truck arrived at the local grocery stores with the regular egg deliveries, they were turned away. Local businesses refused to process Koinonia corn or cotton to make it ready to sell. They couldn't prevent travelers or people from other parts of the country from stopping at the market, so they took to driving past it at night, riddling it with gunfire, shooting holes in the refrigerator and freezer so the meat and the eggs and the milk would go bad. One night some men threw a dozen sticks of dynamite through the doorway. The front side of the stand, the roof, and the floor were blown away. Koinonia rebuilt the stand, but a few months later the people came back and burned it to the ground. This time the Koinonians didn't rebuild. Now there was nowhere to sell the farm produce.

By 1957 the pecan trees that Clarence and Martin had planted when they first arrived had matured and were producing. Clarence got an idea. If the local people wouldn't buy their produce, Koinonia had friends in other parts of the country who would. He would start a mail-order business. Pecans stay fresh for months, shelled or unshelled. So do peanuts. They could be harvested and then shipped whenever there was an order. And the federal post office couldn't refuse to do business with Koinonia. So they advertised the peanuts and pecans, with the marketing slogan, "Help us ship the nuts out of Georgia." People across the country mailed in their orders. Koinonia expanded the mail order business to include fruit cakes, which also keep well, and a cook book. The orders kept coming in. It looked like Koinonia was back in business, on a much smaller scale than before, but it was enough to keep going.

The local citizens saw that their boycott of Koinonia produce didn't seem to be closing the community down, so they decided on a second kind of boycott, a kind of reverse boycott. One day Clarence went into town to buy seed. The merchant said he couldn't sell him any seed. Clarence was surprised. Why not? Because of Clarence's views on racial integration. If Clarence would run an ad in the Americus newspaper renouncing his views on integration, the merchant would sell him anything in the store. Clarence was taken aback for a minute; to renounce his views on racial equality would be to betray his deepest convictions. He couldn't do that. He tried to defuse the situation with humor. "There must be some kind of misunderstanding," he said. "I came in here to buy seed, not to sell my soul." The storekeeper was not amused, and Clarence didn't get the seed. Nobody in town would sell him seed. He had to drive all the way down to Albany, forty miles away, to buy the seed he needed.

It turned out that all the merchants in Americus had decided not to sell anything to Koinonia members. No farm equipment, no fertilizer, no seed, no fuel. No clothes, no medicines, no groceries. The one storekeeper in Americus who bucked the boycott and continued to sell to Koinonia members, Mr. Birdsey, had his store bombed and had to close it anyway. Koinonia members had to drive all the way to Albany to buy anything they couldn't raise on the farm, hoping they had enough gas to get there.

More hardship came. The insurance companies cancelled insurance on Koinonia property, so when anything was destroyed there was no insurance to pay for it. And there was increasing destruction. A series of petty vandalisms began: people would sneak onto the grounds at night to tear down fences so the hogs would get loose. They cut down fruit trees and pecan trees. They peppered the farm vehicles with gunshot. Then the bank closed the Koinonia account. That was in the days before credit cards, and people either wrote checks or paid in cash for anything they bought. Now Clarence had no place in town to cash the checks or deposit the money Koinonia made from the mail order business, and no way to write a check himself. Clarence had to open an account in a bank down in Albany.

The white citizens of Americus and Sumter County hoped that all of this economic pressure would force Koinonia to close, but Clarence had too much stick-to-it-iveness to give up. Besides, they hadn't started the farm for the purpose of making money. They had started it to be a witness to how God wanted people to live. God didn't want people to cut and run when times got hard. And they soon got even harder.

The Ku Klux Klan held a huge rally in a field outside Americus, burning tall wooden crosses and stirring themselves up into greater and greater anger and hatred. They got into their cars and drove to Koinonia in a long seventy-car cavalcade. They slowly and silently drove past the fields, onto the property, around the property, and back out. The intent was to frighten the Koinonia members, to let them know how big the Klan was and that the Klan had their eye on Koinonia. A few days later two members of the Klan arrived at Koinonia and asked to see Clarence. They said they wanted to buy the farm, offering half what the farm was worth. Clarence said the farm was not for sale. Pretending they were concerned about the Jordans' safety, the men pointed out that they were putting their lives in danger by staying there. Florence, who had come out to join Clarence, said, "Then we will not be the first Christians to die for our beliefs nor will we be the last." The men drove away, but a few days later another, larger, group of men came and again offered to buy the farm, again asking that Koinonia members leave. Again they refused.

The national news media had gotten wind of the rally and sent reporters to cover it. The next week pictures of the long, ominous Klan cavalcade driving down the road to Koinonia appeared in two of the biggest news magazines of the day, *Life* and *Look*. Florence later surmised that the national attention probably helped save their lives.

But the local white citizens grew more uncomfortable having a racially integrated community down the road from them, even if they were peaceful and mostly kept to themselves. They couldn't ignore the fact that people kept driving through town on their way to visit Koinonia, some just to visit but some staying to live there. If the Koinonians couldn't be bought off, and if they couldn't be run off through economic hardship or by the threat of danger, the citizens of Sumter County figured they'd have to resort to actual physical violence. Before, they had done drive-by shootings only at the market out on the highway and only at night, when no people would be there. But now they started driving past the Koinonia houses, shooting at them when there were people inside. One day they fired shots at a group of children who were playing volleyball in the open yard, sending them flying into one of the houses, hiding under beds and in closets. And one night when Eleanor was home from college, she and Clarence were sitting and visiting in the living room of the Jordans' house. She got up to get ready for bed and went into her bedroom. Clarence stood up. At that moment a bullet came through the window, passed over the chair where Clarence had been sitting, went into Eleanor's bedroom, passed just over her shoulder and shattered the mirror of the chest of drawers where she was standing. Both Clarence and Eleanor could easily have been killed.

One of the Jordan children, Jan, was later to say that the younger children didn't realize that the reason the adults began to stack wood up around the houses was to stop bullets. They thought they were just bringing in firewood. The grown-ups didn't want to frighten the children, but they taught them to be careful. If a car came down the highway and slowed down, they were to go and stand behind the nearest tree. If they were inside and heard gun-shots they were to drop to the floor. Otherwise they tried to make it possible for the children to lead normal lives.

The black people in Americus or around Sumter County who had been friends with Koinonia realized that their lives were in danger too. Shots were fired into their houses, and crosses were burned in their yards. A fire was set on the front porch of one family, but luckily they were able to put it out before it burned the whole house down. It became unsafe for black people even to speak the name of Koinonia.

When Clarence saw the danger their black friends were in, he told them he understood if they stayed away from the farm and many did, but a few brave souls con-tinued to work at Koinonia anyway and did what they could to help out. Carranza Morgan, whose wife contin-ued working at Koinonia, would drive his truck down to Albany, load it up with fertilizer, and bring it to Koinonia at night. He knew his life was in danger if he got caught, but he did it anyway.

Clarence and Florence and the other adults could try to make life happy for the children on the farm, but they couldn't stop the way the children began to be treated at school. By this time Eleanor was away in college, Jim was in high school, and Jan was in middle school. Lenny, only four, wasn't in school yet. All the Koinonia kids—the Brownes, the Wittkampers, all of them—began to be shunned at school. Their classmates, even the ones who had been their friends, stopped speaking to them. They wouldn't sit with them in the lunch room; if one of the Koinonia children tried to join them, they would pick up their trays and move to another table. In high school the real bullying began. They called the Koinonia kids ugly names and threw spitballs and paper clips at them when the teacher wasn't looking. They came up behind them in the hall and popped them with a rubber band, hard. The older boys were often pushed or hit or knocked around on the school yard. One day a boy threw a knife into the floor right by Jim's foot.

The bullying at school and the drive-by shootings at the farm forced the Koinonia parents to make a hard decision, whether to stay and stand up for what they believed in or leave because their children were in danger. The black families living at Koinonia were in the greatest danger. One family moved out into the nearby countryside, and the other went to live with friends of Koinonia in New Jersey. One by one, many of the white families made the painful decision to leave as well. At the end of the 1950s only three families with children remained at Koinonia: the Jordans, the Brownes, and the Wittkampers. One other couple, Christian and Jeannette Drescher, who were older and had no children living with them, also stayed.

The adults felt that they could make the decision to stay for themselves, but they gave the children a choice; they could stay or go live with friends of the community up north. All nine of the children initially decided to stay and tough it out. But the pressure on Jim, the oldest Jordan son, became so intense that finally they decided that Jim should go stay with friends in North Dakota to finish high school.

## 9

# New Directions

By 1959 THE BOYCOTT had forced Koinonia to give up farming most of the land; there was no local market for the produce. Some mornings Clarence would saddle Star or Danny and ride out over the empty fields. He would get off the horse, scoop up a little dirt and turn it over in his hand. He had worked so hard to make that soil fertile and rich. He had loved that land. He had poured his life into it. It had been a farm dedicated to God and God's kingdom. How had it come to such failure? How had *he* come to such failure? Why had the people in Sumter County come to hate him so much and to hate what he stood for? Everybody wants to be loved, Clarence mused. All his life he had been loved. Even when people disagreed with him or when he disagreed with them, they still loved him. And he still loved them. But he wasn't loved now, at least not in Sumter County. He was actually hated; even his children were hated because of him. It was very hard to take it in.

But at least the physical violence against the farm died down. Night after night passed with no drive-by shootings;

no mornings of waking up to find fences torn down and the hogs running loose on the highway, or to find fruit trees and pecan trees cut off at the base. A cautious feeling of safety set in, but only on the farm. The safety didn't extend to town or the local schools. Koinonia members were still not safe on the streets of Americus. One day Con Browne was delivering mail orders to the railway express office. He had unloaded the back of the station wagon and returned to the car for packages in the front seat when he was suddenly attacked by a large, heavy-set man, who hit Con in the face with such force that it sent Con reeling back into the front seat of the car. The man continued to pummel Con, shouting angry words at him. Then, just as suddenly, he disappeared, leaving Con bleeding from his face and nose and with deep bruises on his body. The police did nothing to investigate the attack.

Koinonia kids continued to be harassed and bullied at school; Greg Wittkamper was later to say that they were like soldiers on the battlefront. But they did their best to ignore the bullying and not fight back, and at least when they came home they were safe.

The community did continue to grow some field crops: peanuts, corn, and several acres of muscadine grapes, which were Clarence's pride and joy. They were harvested in August and loaded into the farm's old dump truck to be delivered to Atlanta to sell. People from around the country who had heard Clarence speak rallied to support the struggling community. The mail order business began to boom. Pecans, harvested by the truckload, were brought to the pecan plant to be cracked and shelled. Extra workers were hired. Women with white bib aprons and hair nets sat at long metal tables. They carefully removed any remaining bits of shell from the perfectly formed pecan halves, which were then packed into one-pound cellophane bags or half-pound cardboard boxes or two-and-a-half-pound metal tins. Defective or discolored pieces were discarded, while broken halves or smaller pieces were packaged or put aside for use in fruitcake or chocolate candy.

The delicious aromas coming from the fruitcake and candy kitchen in the adjacent building were too tempting for the workers in the office not to go over occasionally for a nibble or two. Clarence, working with a local woman, Willa Mae Champion, developed a secret recipe for fruitcake. And sometimes when the candy making was at its peak, hands in the office or shipping room were happy to stop their paperwork on a minute's notice to run over to help spread the warm mixture evenly on marble slabs.

The mail order business was expanded to include tie-dyed clothing, peasant dresses for women and girls, and handmade pottery. And there were still streams of visitors to Koinonia–eight or nine hundred people a year. Young people from colleges and universities, members of the clergy, newspaper and magazine reporters looking for an unusual story, even dignitaries like the Dean of the Harvard Divinity School and a member of the Japanese Parliament, all interested in Clarence's dream. There were even homeless "drifters" who showed up. Clarence greeted each visitor kindly, taking them about the property, explaining what the community was intended to be. People marveled that in spite of all that he had suffered Clarence was still the same kind, gentle, humorous person he had always been. But beneath it all at times he felt discouraged and at a loss for direction.

Florence knew they had to be prepared at a moment's notice to provide hospitality for unexpected visitors. On her weekly trips to Albany for groceries she would wait until the turkeys were on sale and buy several, which she took home to freeze. When she heard that a large group of visitors were coming, she'd thaw a turkey and put the word out to the other households to make side dishes—and the visitors would share a Thanksgiving feast.

With the visitors sometimes pitching in to help, there were plenty of adults to keep the mail order business going, take care of the children, farm the crops, cook the meals, and maintain the property. Now something that had been in the back of Clarence's mind for some time came simmering to the surface. To understand it we have to go all the way back to the early days of Koinonia, and even before that, to his seminary days.

Ever since the founding of Koinonia, Clarence had been invited to speak at other places–sometimes at churches or church conferences, sometimes at colleges or universities. Most preachers, when they go out to preach or teach, carry their Bibles with them. They find the passage they want to preach or teach on, read it aloud, and then elaborate on what the passage said. Clarence carried his Bible with him too–but his Bible was not written in English, it was written in Greek. He would open up that Greek Bible, and translate the passage into English as he read. Clarence had fallen in love with reading the Bible in the original Greek when he was in seminary, because he wanted to get the message "straight from the stream," as he put it, not in the English of another time period, or as other people had translated it.

For Clarence, the Bible related directly to his own life and time. He wanted other people to see it that way too, not as a history of some remote time and place. So he began to tell the stories from the Bible as if they had taken place right there in rural Georgia in the twentieth century. He told about Jesus' disciple Peter. When Peter was born, he had been named Simon bar-Jonah, but Jesus had renamed him, calling him Peter, which means "rock" in Greek. "Bar-Jonah" means "son of John." So Clarence called him Rock Johnson. Peter had a brother, Andrew. Together they were Rock and Andy Johnson—that's what they would have been called in twentieth-century Georgia, at least. And that's what Clarence called them.

Nazareth would have been like the little town of Valdosta, in south Georgia. So that's where Clarence had Mary living when the Angel Gabriel appeared to her to tell her she was to give birth to Jesus. Jerusalem would be . . . well, it would be the capital city of Georgia—Atlanta. The story of the Good Samaritan, the outcast who was the only one who would help a man who had been wounded and robbed and left by the roadside? In Georgia in Clarence's time, that outcast person would be a black man. And that's the way Clarence told the story.

Clarence's audiences loved the stories. He called them the "cotton patch" version of the Gospel. They went over so well that people began to urge him to write out the entire New Testament in "cotton patch" style and have it published as a book. The idea kept coming back to him, and now that there wasn't as much work to do on the farm, it seemed like the time to begin.

He knew he would need a quiet place to write, away from the hubbub of community life. He picked out a spot back at the edge of the pecan orchard and built a little wooden shack, with a roof, a door, a rough wooden floor, and a couple of windows. He moved a desk and a chair in there and began to write.

It would have seemed that Clarence would begin with the Gospels, the books that told the stories of Jesus' life. But somehow Clarence was drawn to the letters of St. Paul. For someone who didn't know what Clarence was going through, that might have seemed a strange choice. But Clarence had a lot in common with St. Paul. Paul was a follower of Jesus in the first century who traveled around teaching about Jesus in various places and drawing people together to form churches. As he continued to travel, he would write letters back to the churches he had established. The letters were full of instruction and spiritual insight. They also reflected some of Paul's own struggles and difficulties.

Paul's understanding of Jesus' message had made him as much of an outcast in his day as Clarence was in his. Like Clarence, Paul was a man whose heart, whose mind, whose whole being had been captivated by Jesus. Paul had been a part of an elite Jewish sect, the Pharisees, but had given up the status and privilege that came with being a Pharisee to become a follower of Jesus. Clarence had been a member of an old established white Southern family and a minister in the largest denomination in the South. He had given up status and privilege to follow Jesus too. In Paul's day, the Jewish people thought that God's favor was for them alone. The disturbing message that Paul preached was that God was also reaching out to the non-Jewish people, the Gentiles—and he went so far as to say that there was no distinction between Jews and Gentiles in God's family. That was as disturbing back in the first century as Clarence's message of racial equality was in the 20th. And Paul had suffered much as Clarence had for standing up for his beliefs—more so, in fact. Paul had been thrown out of the Jewish synagogues, he had been stoned, and finally he had been put in prison and killed because people didn't want to hear what he said about God and the way God wanted people to live. Clarence had been put out of churches too. He hadn't been stoned, but he had been shot at, and it was just a miracle that he hadn't been killed. For Clarence, exploring Paul's suffering and trying to express Paul's message in "cotton patch" terms was a connection with a kindred spirit over a two-thousand-year span. Translating Paul's words into his own present-day situation gave Clarence a kind of comfort and assurance he needed.

In the mid-1960s, some of the long-time members of Koinonia began to feel that they weren't really needed anymore, that they should go where their particular gifts to serve God could be used. Within a few months of each other, the Dreschers left to join a community in Alabama and the Brownes left when Con was offered a position at the Highlander Folk School in Tennessee. That left the Jordans and the Wittkampers as the only permanent resident families. But people kept coming. One such couple were Al and Carol Henry. Al had been pastor of a church in

Birmingham, Alabama; he had been fired for preaching a sermon advocating racial integration. Al and Carol came to Koinonia seeking people with a common vision, but their presence at Koinonia was to bring greater blessing than they could have imagined.

As Linda Fuller has described in her Foreword, one December day Al got a phone call from an old friend, Millard Fuller. Millard and his wife Linda and their two children, Chris and Kim, had been on a family trip in Florida and were on their way back home to Montgomery, Alabama. They had stopped for breakfast in Albany, when Millard remembered that Al and Carol had moved to a community somewhere in Georgia. With the telephone operator's help, Millard located Al and Carol at Koinonia, just forty miles away. Al invited them to come up for a visit. Millard and Linda had planned to stop by briefly and be on their way home, but the Henrys persuaded them to stay for lunch. They were glad they did.

The dining hall was abuzz with people dusting off their hands, then washing them at the sink near the door, getting in line to serve their plates, picking up glasses of iced tea or water, finding a place at a table to sit. The Henrys and the Fullers served their plates and sat down on some apple crates at a long table. Two other visitors were already sitting there, a newspaper reporter from Columbus, Georgia, and a retired Navy chaplain who were there to interview Clarence. In a minute Clarence walked in. Al Henry nudged Millard. "That's Clarence Jordan," he whispered. Clarence spotted the reporter and the chaplain, served his plate, and sat down at the long table, next to Millard and Linda and across from the two men.

They began peppering Clarence with questions about war and peace and racial justice. Millard and Linda listened, amazed at Clarence's answers. As Millard later recalled, "When Clarence walked in, I thought he looked like a typical south Georgia farmer, but he sure didn't talk like a typical south Georgia farmer." Millard and Linda found Clarence's answers to the two men's questions the most profound they had ever heard.

Finally Clarence and the two men turned to Millard and Linda. Who were they and what had brought them to Koinonia? Millard and Linda explained that they were on a family trip, looking for a new direction in their lives. Millard had made millions of dollars as a businessman and a lawyer, but in the process he had neglected his family. He spent little time with Linda and the children. Finally Linda had left him and had gone up to New York City to seek counsel with a minister there. Millard had pursued her and begged her to come back. She said she would, if they would seek a new direction for their lives. Millard agreed. They had come home to Alabama, packed their Lincoln Continental, and, with their two children, set out on a family vacation to Florida. They needed some family time, and also time away to start thinking and praying about what God might have them do with their lives. And here they were.

After lunch, Millard drew Linda aside for a brief conversation, and they approached Clarence. "We came here expecting to stay less than an hour," Millard said, "but we'd like to stay longer if you'll have us." Clarence said they were welcome to stay. There was even a house they could move into. Millard and Linda looked at the house; Millard later joked that it seemed to be about the size of the Lincoln Continental they had driven up in—a tiny house, three or four hundred square feet in size, with one space heater, for all four of them. Millard and Linda gulped a few times and said, "Okay. We'll stay."

Millard wanted to spend as much time as he could with Clarence. One of Clarence's jobs was to milk the cow every morning; Millard signed on as his helper. They'd carry two stools into the barn, and one bucket. One

would sit on one side of the cow and the other on the other side, and begin to milk. Millard would ask Clarence a question and Clarence would answer, and pretty soon they'd be leaning over, talking to each other between the cow's hind legs and her tail, still squirting milk into the bucket. Millard learned so much about Jesus in the cow barn that he later told people he had been to seminary at Cow University.

When Clarence went to help ship orders, Millard would join him, and pretty soon they'd be leaning back, propping their feet up on the table and talking about Jesus. "Clarence, I feel bad about interrupting you," Millard once said. "I offered to help and I'm just interrupting your work."

"That's okay. People are more important than pecans," Clarence said, and they'd go right on talking.

Millard and Linda stayed a month, through Christmas-time. Winter weather set in, and the one unvented gas heater in the Fullers' house couldn't be left on all night with the doors and windows closed. All the oxygen would be sucked out of the air or the flames would go out and the family would die. So it got really cold at night. Florence made sure they had plenty of blankets, but Chris and Kim complained that their ears got cold. Florence got out her sewing machine and made two little cotton flannel "pixie" hats, pointed at the top with ties keeping them snugly on the children's heads. Now Chris and Kim could pretend to be elves as they drifted off to sleep under their warm blankets.

In January the word came to Millard that Tougaloo College, a predominantly black college in Mississippi, needed someone to help with publicity and to raise money for a badly needed dormitory. That was the kind of thing Millard knew he could do well, and he took the job.

Now the empty fields began to weigh more heavily on Clarence. All that land just going to waste. Maybe God was calling him in a new direction, maybe a new ministry of preaching and teaching, based up around Atlanta. He and Florence talked with Margaret and Will Wittkamper about selling or giving away the Koinonia property and moving on. The Wittkampers disagreed; they wanted to stay. Koinonia was home. So the Jordans agreed to stay. Clarence continued to work on his Cotton Patch versions of the Bible, to accept speaking engagements and help with community chores, but he felt like he had lost a central direction for his life, a burning sense of purpose. It seemed to him that Koinonia had failed and that it was time to give up and move away.

There was one bright spot during those years: Association Press in New York had accepted Clarence's Cotton Patch Version of Paul's Epistles for publication. Now he turned to writing Cotton Patch Versions of the four Gospels. But still the days and weeks and months seemed to drag on. Then one day he got a two-sentence letter from Millard, "I have resigned my position at Tougaloo. What have you got up your sleeve?"

Clarence didn't feel that he had anything "up his sleeve" except the Cotton Patch Gospels. He wrote Millard back that maybe there was something up God's sleeve for them to do together. The Fullers, now with their third child, Faith, moved back to Koinonia on a more permanent basis in early 1968, and Millard and Clarence put their heads together. The plan they came up with was eventually to make Clarence's dreams for helping poor people have a better life come true on a scale he never even hoped could be possible.

## 10

# An Ending—and a Beginning

WHEN CLARENCE AND MILLARD put their heads together, the ideas started to fly. Clarence would continue to teach and to write the Cotton Patch versions of the Bible, that much was clear. But was there any reason to stay on the farm? They still believed in living in community and shared the dream of helping poor people live better lives. But how were they to do that? The days of share cropping were coming to an end, as big machines did the work formerly done by human hands. Maybe they should move to a city. But as Millard and Clarence drove around the countryside, they saw that even though share-cropping days were over, a lot of people were still living in share-cropper houses, tumble-down shacks with no electricity or running water. How could a person have any self-respect, living in a house like that? Maybe Koinonia could find a way to improve people's living conditions through building decent houses.

The more they thought about it, the more they began to see a new direction for Koinonia. The "new" Koinonia would maintain the old principles of living in community, but the focus would be on outreach ministries. They saw themselves as being in partnership with God, carrying out God's plans on earth, as well as being in partnership with humankind; it would be a way that people with more resources could partner with people who had less. Clarence wrote a letter to the hundreds of friends on the Koinonia mailing list, telling them of the plan, which they called Koinonia Partners. One aspect of the new vision, the one that really took off, they called Partnership Housing. The more Clarence and Millard talked about Partnership Housing, the more excited they got. What poor people needed, Clarence said, was a hand-up, not a hand-out. It wouldn't be a give-away program. They didn't see themselves building houses *for* people; they would involve the people themselves in building the houses, as partners in the project. The owners of the first house would turn around and help build the second house, and so on. That way they could build simple, sturdy houses at a very low cost. The family who would own the house would pay for it over time, but only the cost of the house itself; they wouldn't have to pay interest on the money, the way banks charged. But where would they build the houses? That's when they realized that they had what they needed right there–land, plenty of land. They didn't need to move at all.

They didn't have a lot of money to start such an enterprise, but they started with what money they had, calling it the Fund for Humanity, and soon contributions started to roll in from Koinonia friends across the country. This was in the days of the "hippie" movement, when many young people were seeking ways to live simply and peacefully. Families as well as individuals flocked to Koinonia to see what was happening. As before, some stayed for a few days or weeks, and others stayed on to become Koinonia Partners. Some worked at farming, some at clearing land for the new Partnership houses, some at developing small industries, like the sewing industry.

Weekdays would begin with the adults gathering at 7:30 a.m. for devotions. Clarence would lead the Bible study, often based on a passage he had translated the day before from the Greek, making it relevant to their everyday lives. After a morning of work, lunch would be shared in the community dining room, and only bad weather prevented a volleyball game in the quadrangle after lunch. Work resumed about 2 p.m.

For the Partnership Housing project, they sectioned off forty-two half-acre lots along the northern boundary of the farm, and set aside a four-acre plot to be a playground and family recreation area. Then they put the word out about Partnership Housing. Bo and Emma Johnson signed up for the first house. Bo and Emma seemed like the perfect choice: Clarence and Florence had known the Johnsons since the early days of Koinonia and Bo had worked on the farm over the years. The concrete slab was poured and in a few days the walls were being framed. Soon Bo and Emma and their children would have a decent house to live in.

Koinonia was headed in its new direction. Clarence felt a happiness he hadn't known for years. Everything seemed to be looking up. His three oldest children had graduated from college and Lenny was a senior in high school; he'd be off to college next year. They had all made it through the hard years safely. Millard and Linda and their children were a source of unbounded joy; their very presence gave Clarence hope for the future.

For Linda, one of the highlights of that year was manually typing Clarence's final manuscript of Luke and Acts to be sent to the publisher. In those days before computers and electronic transmission, it took much longer for a book to be published. It was almost a year later that the book came off the press and the first copies arrived at Koinonia. Clarence began signing them and gave Millard and Linda one of the first autographed copies.

By then, he had gotten a good start on the Cotton Patch version of John's Gospel. And it seemed that there were some people in Georgia who wanted to hear Clarence's message after all; he had spoken to a large conference in Atlanta the past May and was invited to preach a sermon at Mercer University, the largest Baptist university in Georgia, in early November. But in the last few days of October, the week before he was to go to Mercer to deliver the sermon, Clarence began to feel a bit ill–aches and pains and a low fever. He thought he had the flu and took it easy for a few days, but then on Wednesday afternoon of that week he felt a bit better and thought he'd better get to work on that sermon.

The walk to the writing shack seemed longer than usual, and Clarence was tired when he got there, but he sat down and began to write. In a little while he heard a light tap at the door. It was Lena Hofer, a young woman who had joined the community several months before. She apologized for interrupting Clarence but she just had to tell him about a project at school that had gone well and she wanted some advice about a letter she had received from home. Clarence gave her his full attention, as he gave all his guests. He offered her advice about the letter, and as she was saying good-bye, she saw Clarence's body give a strange jerk. His head fell back against the wall and his arms dropped to his side. She seized his head in her hands and called his name, but got no response. She knew she needed to get help and, giving Clarence one last desperate look, ran as fast as she could up to the community yard. Lenny was the first person she saw. "Something is wrong with your dad," she shouted, her arms flailing, and kept running to find Florence.

Lenny jumped in the station wagon and sped down to the writing shack. He took one look at his father and began to give him mouth-to-mouth resuscitation, trying to breathe air back into Clarence's lungs to revive him. But it was no use. Clarence didn't respond. Meanwhile Lena had reached Florence and Millard and Al Zook, another member of the community. They were on their way down to the writing shack when Lenny met them on the way. "It's too late," he said. "He's dead."

The community was in shock. Clarence was only fifty-seven years old, and except for his cold he seemed to be in the peak of health. The new directions for Koinonia had been under way for only a year. But they did know that Clarence would have wanted a simple funeral. They found a plain pine box for a casket and buried Clarence's body the next day, up on Picnic Hill. About seventy-five people had gathered, some dressed in suits and hats and high heels and some barefoot in dusty working clothes. Millard read some verses from Clarence's version of 1 Peter and 1 John (called 1 Rock and 1 Jack in the Cotton Patch versions). The first four verses of I Jack read,

> In order that you all too might be our partners, we're plainly telling you about something that's real, something that we ourselves have heard, that we have seen with our own two eyes. It's about the idea of life which we looked at and even felt of with our own hands. Now the life took shape and we saw it, and we are giving you our word and plainly telling you about the spiritual life which was with

the Father and which took shape in front of us.
Our partnership, then, is with the Father and with
his son Jesus Christ. And we are recording this so
that the joy of us all may be completely full.

The men lowered the coffin into the grave, and when they began to shovel dirt on top of it, Faith Fuller, who was two, stepped to the edge of the grave and sang, "Happy birthday to you happy birthday to you, happy birthday, dear Clarence, happy birthday to you." It surprised everybody, but then they realized it was just right. Clarence was passing on to a new life.

∽

After Clarence's death, nobody even considered stopping the work he had begun. Koinonia must go on. Bo and Emma Johnson's house was completed, and others were started. Increasing numbers of people came to visit or to join the community. New books and old audio recordings of Clarence's teachings were added to the list of Koinonia products. Contributions to the Fund for Humanity continued to come in, financing the building of a dozen houses in the next two years.

By 1972, with twenty-five families moved out of shacks into decent houses, Millard and Linda began to think about taking the partnership housing idea overseas. They left to go build houses with poor people in Africa. Three years later they returned and proposed that Koinonia take the partnership housing idea beyond the boundaries of the farm to a national and even an international level. Florence and the other members of the community thought about it and decided that Koinonia should not take on such a large-scale project; Koinonia should remain a local enterprise. They gave Millard and Linda their support and their blessing, and right there at Koinonia Millard and Linda set up a couple of desks, a typewriter, and a telephone to begin a ministry they called Habitat for Humanity.

Just as Koinonia Partners had, Habitat for Humanity grew at a phenomenal pace. The Fullers, along with an increasing number of mostly volunteer staff, devoted themselves to Habitat based on commitment to the mission rather than financial compensation. Habitat continued the work in Africa, and the first U.S. house was completed in San Antonio, Texas, in 1979, ten years after Clarence's death. Another ten years would see the completion of the ten thousandth Habitat house, in nearby Atlanta. By the year 2000, Millard was calculating that Habitat was completing twenty-six houses per day worldwide. In the thirty-eight years since its founding, Habitat for Humanity has built more than five hundred thousand houses around the world, providing decent homes for more than two and a half million people.

In his early years at Koinonia, Clarence had known success and prosperity and hope and joy. In later years he knew hatred and rejection and violence and deep sadness. But he had held on—that old stick-to-it-iveness served him well. And finally, just when he was so discouraged he was ready to give up, along came a new direction that turned his dreams into a reality greater than he had ever imagined.

# Epilogue

## The Future of a Dream

IN THE FORTY-SIX YEARS since Clarence's death, Koinonia has seen many changes. The flood of visitors didn't just continue—it grew. Thousands of people from all around the world and from all walks of life have come to Koinonia, some to stay for a day or two, some for longer visits, some to join the community and to stay for many years. Some have been young, some have been old, some have brought children with them, and some have had children born there.

Florence lived for eighteen years after Clarence's death, a source of love and wisdom and strength to members and visitors alike. She was famous for the beautiful wedding cakes she baked for the marriages that took place in the community and the tea and freshly baked cookies that welcomed people, young and old, for a visit on her screened porch.

Habitat for Humanity wasn't the only ministry that was to grow out of Koinonia. Clarence's vision for community living was the inspiration for four other communities founded in the 1970s: Laestare Partners in Rockford, Illinois; Friendship House in Boise, Idaho; Jubilee Partners near Comer, Georgia; and New Hope House near Griffin, Georgia. Each community has its own distinct style and mission. For example, Jubilee Partners reaches out to people who have escaped hardship or oppression in their native lands, seeking safety in America; New Hope House provides hospitality for people who are visiting relatives incarcerated in a nearby prison. In 2005, Millard and Linda Fuller founded The Fuller Center for Housing, which sustains the principles that guided the formation of Koinonia's Partnership Housing and the founding of Habitat for Humanity.

Clarence's Cotton Patch versions of the Bible are still in print, and many of his sermons and other writings have also been published in books. Some of the talks that he gave were audiotaped, and these have been copied to CD's so that people can listen to his voice today.

In the 1980s a musical version of Clarence's Cotton Patch Version of the Gospels of Matthew and John was produced off Broadway in New York City. Called "The Cotton Patch Gospel," the play was written by Tom Key and Russell Treyz and the music and lyrics were composed by the well-known singer and song-writer Harry Chapin. People have been tapping their feet to the blue-grass songs and listening to Clarence's version of Jesus' teachings in theatres ever since. In 1988, Tom Key produced a video-taped version that has also been seen across the country.

In 2005, Faith Fuller produced a documentary of the history of Koinonia, "Briars in the Cotton Patch," which has been widely aired on public television stations. More recently, in 2010, another play based on Clarence's life, "The Glory Man," was produced at Lamb's Players Theatre in Coronado, California.

The pecan trees that Clarence and Martin planted in 1942 continue to bear fruit. Along with other pecan trees planted in more recent years, they are a staple of the continuing mail order business that still "ships the nuts out of Georgia." Today cattle again graze under the pecan trees, and pigs and goats and chickens enjoy the children who come to visit and feed them. Clarence's writing shack, now empty, still stands along the edge of the pecan orchard; you can go there for a visit. Members of the community and visitors often walk the Peace Trail that winds through the woods, inviting people to reflect on Clarence's dream and how it may meet new challenges today.

The children who grew up at Koinonia in the early days now live in many parts of the country, many of them carrying the scars of having been bullied throughout their years of high school because of theirs and their families' beliefs. Greg Wittkamper and his family live in West Virginia. In 2006 Greg received a surprising letter in the mail. It was from one of his former classmates at Americus High School, who had been one of the students who had made Greg's life so miserable there. He wrote that he was sorry for the way he had treated Greg all those years ago and he was writing to ask Greg to consider coming to the fortieth class reunion. Another letter from another classmate arrived, and then another. They all told Greg they were sorry and hoped that he might forgive them and come to the reunion. It was a difficult decision for Greg, to go back to that place where he had experienced so much pain, but in the end he decided to go and it turned out to be a week-end of deep reconciliation and healing of past hurts. Greg's story, told by Jim Auchmutey, was recently published under the title *The Class of '65: A Student, A Divided Town and the Long Road to Forgiveness*. Beverly England Williams's biography of her parents has also recently been published, titled *By Faith and By Love: Martin and Mabel's Journey*.

Great progress has been made in relations with the local community. Hatred against Koinonia has died down over the years, and today the community enjoys a safe and peaceful existence. The Americus Ministerial Association now includes both black and white members. A breakthrough came in 1997 when Norris Harris, an African-American minister long associated with Koinonia, was invited to speak to the "all-white" First Baptist Church in Americus. As Norris said, "I'm living the future of the dream that Clarence had."

# Author's Note

THIS BOOK HAS BEEN in the making for a long time, though I didn't know it in the beginning! I first heard of Clarence Jordan some 30 years ago, when I was living in Lake Placid, New York, and my pastor recommended the Cotton Patch Gospels to me. I thought they were funny and wise and amazingly original. And maybe they struck a special chord in me since I was a displaced Southerner at the time, having grown up in the Deep South myself.

Then, ten years later, when I was in graduate school at the University of Georgia in Athens, a friend took me to visit Jubilee Partners, an offshoot of Koinonia in nearby Comer. That visit gave me a second glimpse of Clarence and his vision for what Christian community might be. He continued to hover somewhere in the back of my mind, but it was not until 15 years later that I visited Koinonia for the first time. By then I had taken a position on the faculty at Louisiana State University, teaching courses in children's literature. I had been visiting family members in Atlanta and decided to stop by Koinonia for a night or two on the way home to see it for myself.

At that time Dave and Ellie Castle were members of the community. Dave gave the small group of us who were first-time visitors a tour of the farm and that evening showed us Faith Fuller's documentary of the history of Koinonia, "Briars in the Cottonpatch." The film is very powerful, showing many of the wonderful moments the community has enjoyed and many of the frightening, cruel things that happened too, ending with Clarence's death. Dave turned off the DVD player. "He was a great man," Dave said. "A pioneer of Civil Rights. But nobody will ever hear of him."

Dave's words cut me to the heart. "Children need to know this story," a voice in me said. "Clarence's story needs to be written for children." I decided that I would try. And so I set out to learn everything I could about Clarence. I read all the books I could get my hands on: Dallas Lee's and Ann Louise Coble's biographies of Clarence, *Cotton Patch Evidence* and *Cotton Patch for the Kingdom* and Tracy K'Meyer's *Interracialism and Christian Community in the Postwar South*. I read *Koinonia Remembered*, a compilation of many people's memories of living in the community over the years. To make sure I had a good sense of Clarence's understanding of the Gospel, I read all of his published works I could find and listened to CD's of his teachings on the parables and on peace that were not in print. I interviewed Millard Fuller about his years at Koinonia and his deep friendship with Clarence. I read biographies and autobiographies of Millard, including his *Love in the Mortar Joints* and *Beyond the American Dream* and Bettie B. Young's *The House that Love Built*. I also read

Millard's *Building Materials for Life* series, in which he relates anecdotes about Clarence.

Bren Dubay, executive director of Koinonia, graciously gave me access to the community archives, where I spent days going through original documents, photographs, and newspaper clippings. I interviewed members of the community, some of whom had known Clarence but most of whom had joined the community after his death. They were able to fill in many details about the history and current operation of the farm. One of the members found a long-forgotten audiotape of an interview with Frank Jordan, Clarence's brother. On the tape, Frank relates his memories of growing up with Clarence, telling stories about Clarence's boyhood that only a brother or sister would know. Frank's memories shaped the first chapter of this book. Jim Jordan and Suzan Kezim, Eleanor's daughter, read the manuscript and were able to give me valuable new perspectives.

I spent most of a day reading through the Clarence Jordan papers at the Hargrett Library at the University of Georgia. Along with newsletters, photographs, newspaper clippings and other memorabilia, I found hundreds of letters of support that Clarence and the community had received over the years from all parts of the United States, along with the flood of letters and telegrams following his death, including one from Coretta Scott King.

In the fall of 2012 I attended the Clarence Jordan Symposium in Americus, celebrating the 100th anniversary of Clarence's birth and the 70th anniversary of the founding of Koinonia. Many people, including Linda Fuller Degelmann and Greg Wittkamper, were there to speak of their memories of Clarence and of living at Koinonia. As this book was nearing publication, Linda graciously agreed to write the Foreword and shared with me her still-fresh memories of Clarence and Florence and Koinonia during the times she and Millard lived there. Her interest and support have been invaluable.

Somewhere along the way, the "children" for whom I wanted to write grew up. The book is now intended for young people ages 10 and up. And somewhere along the way I came to love the man whose story I was writing. Rarely have I encountered a person of such grace and humor and faith and intelligence and courage and loving-kindness, all rolled into one. It is my hope that his story will give its readers pleasure and hope, and a sense of the kind of life it is possible to live. Writing it has been joyful, holy work.

In writing Clarence's story, I have wanted to serve the purposes of good biography and good literary storytelling: to present a life accurately while making it engaging to the reader. All of the people in the story, all of the incidents, are based on historical record or personal memories. I have added a few sensory details of setting—summer heat, flies buzzing, a cool breeze—that I, a Southerner myself, sense must have been present, and which I hope give the reader a more immediate sense of what Clarence would have experienced.

In the bibliography I have provided a list of recommended books, DVD's and CD's for further reading, viewing and listening. They are widely available, many of them through Koinonia's website, www.koinoniafarm.org.

# Acknowledgements

Many people have provided encouragement and support for the writing of this book, but there are several people whose help I particularly acknowledge. First, Katherine Thomas, who served as my consultant for the book, raising important questions and providing insight and encouragement, along with her family, Susie, Britt, and Olivia. I am grateful for the late Millard Fuller and Linda Fuller Degelmann, whose memories, perspectives, and encouragement have been invaluable; for Bren Dubay, Director of Koinonia Farm and other members of Koinonia for their generosity through interviews and access to Koinoia archives; and for the Jordan family and particularly Jim Jordan and for reading the manuscript and providing refinements of detail and perspective.

I extend thanks to the Continuing Community circle at the Red Shoes in Baton Rouge, and especially to Grace Ramke; to my children's literature group, Jacqueline Bach, Barbara Benton, Charity Cantey, Renee Casbergue, Karen Donnelly, Tad Hardy, and Elizabeth Willis, for their helpful feedback on the manuscript; and to Lucy Parlange, Randy Harelson, MaryKatherine Callaway, and Jim Auchmutey for their ongoing interest and encouragement.

# Bibliography

## Books by Clarence Jordan

Jordan, Clarence. *Cotton Patch Gospel: The Complete Collection.* Macon, GA: Smyth & Helwys, 2012.

_____. *The Cotton Patch Version of Hebrews and General Epistles.* Clinton, NJ: New Win, 1970.

_____. *The Cotton Patch Version of Luke and Acts: Jesus' Doings and the Happenings.* New York: Association, 1969.

_____. *The Cotton Patch Version of Matthew and John.* New York: Association, 1970.

_____. *The Cotton Patch Version of Paul's Epistles.* Macon, GA: Smyth & Helwys, 1968/2004.

_____. *Sermon on the Mount.* Valley Forge, PA: Valley Forge, PA: Judson, 1952.

_____. *The Substance of Faith and Other Cotton Patch Sermons by Clarence Jordan* (edited by Dallas Lee) New York: Association, 1972.

_____. and Bill Lane Doulos. *Cotton Patch Parables of Liberation.* Scottsdale, PA: Herald, 1976.

## Books about Clarence and Koinonia

Barnette, Henlee, H. *Clarence Jordan: Turning Dreams into Deeds.* Macon, GA: Smyth & Helwys, 1992.

Coble, Ann Louise. *Cotton Patch for the Kingdom: Clarence Jordan's Demonstration Plot at Koinonia Farm.* Scottsdale, PA, Herald, 2002.

Lee, Dallas. *The Cotton Patch Evidence: The Story of Clarence Jordan and the Koinonia Farm Experiment (1942-1970).* Americus, GA: Koinonia, 1971.

Lyman-Barner, Kirk and Cori Lyman-Barner, eds. *Fruits of the Cotton Patch: The Clarence Jordan Symposium 2012, Volume 2.* Eugene, OR: Cascade Books, 2014.

Lyman-Barner, Kirk and Cori Lyman-Barner, eds. *Roots in the Cotton Patch: The Clarence Jordan Symposium 2012, Volume 1.* Eugene, OR: Cascade Books, 2014.

Weiner, Kay N., ed. *Koinonia Remembered: The First Fifty Years.* Americus, GA: Koinonia, 1992.

## Books with a Background of Clarence and Koinonia

Auchmutey, Jim. *The Class of '65: A Student, A Divided Town and the Long Road to Forgiveness.* Public Affairs, 2015.
Williams, Beverly England, *By Faith and by Love: Martin and Mabel's Story.* Wipf and Stock, 2015.

## DVD's

*Briars in the Cottonpatch: The Story of Koinonia Farm.* Cotton Patch Productions, 2003.
*Cotton Patch Gospel* (Tom Key). Bridgestone Productions, 1988.

## CD's

Jordan, Clarence. "The Cotton Patch Parables." Americus, GA: Koinonia Records, nd.
_____. "Christian Pacifism." Americus, GA: Koinonia Partners, nd.
_____. "The Koinonia Story." Americus, GA: Koinonia Partners, nd.
Morrison, Scott. "The Clarence Jordan Interviews." Americus, GA: Koinonia Partners, nd.

Made in the USA
Coppell, TX
28 August 2020

34589901R00069